The LAWS of the UNIVERSE and the BIBLE

A Practical Guide to Abundant Living

LORI KOSTENUK

BALBOA PRESS
A DIVISION OF HAY HOUSE

Copyright © 2016 Lori Kostenuk.

All rights reserved. No part of this book may be used or reproduced by any means, graphic, electronic, or mechanical, including photocopying, recording, taping or by any information storage retrieval system without the written permission of the author except in the case of brief quotations embodied in critical articles and reviews.

Balboa Press books may be ordered through booksellers or by contacting:

Balboa Press
A Division of Hay House
1663 Liberty Drive
Bloomington, IN 47403
www.balboapress.com
1 (877) 407-4847

Because of the dynamic nature of the Internet, any web addresses or links contained in this book may have changed since publication and may no longer be valid. The views expressed in this work are solely those of the author and do not necessarily reflect the views of the publisher, and the publisher hereby disclaims any responsibility for them.

The author of this book does not dispense medical advice or prescribe the use of any technique as a form of treatment for physical, emotional, or medical problems without the advice of a physician, either directly or indirectly. The intent of the author is only to offer information of a general nature to help you in your quest for emotional and spiritual well-being. In the event you use any of the information in this book for yourself, which is your constitutional right, the author and the publisher assume no responsibility for your actions.

Scripture quotations, unless otherwise noted, are from the King James Version of the Bible.

Any people depicted in stock imagery provided by Thinkstock are models, and such images are being used for illustrative purposes only. Certain stock imagery © Thinkstock.

Print information available on the last page.

ISBN: 978-1-5043-5610-7 (sc)
ISBN: 978-1-5043-5612-1 (hc)
ISBN: 978-1-5043-5611-4 (e)

Library of Congress Control Number: 2016906570

Balboa Press rev. date: 08/22/2016

Contents

Foreword vii

Chapter 1 Law of Vibration 1
Chapter 2 Application of the Law of Faith 17
Chapter 3 What Hinders the Law of Faith 71
Chapter 4 Law of Love 88
Chapter 5 Law of Circulation (Flow) 97
Chapter 6 Law of Abundance 113
Chapter 7 Law of Cause and Effect 130
Chapter 8 Law of Detachment 137

Afterword 147
Bibliography 153
About the Author 157

Foreword

I felt humbled when I first set out to write this book. Where do I begin to tell of my own experience of what our family has gleaned from our great Creator and His marvelous ways? To know and understand the energy laws of the universe is to know and understand a little more of the mind of our Creator. My purpose in penning this book is to share with you what I have learned of this metaphysical bridge that connects the spiritual side of our life with the mental and physical sides of our lives—a fusion that completes our whole being.

Our third son was in his late teens when he was completely overwhelmed with seemingly irrational fear and anxiety. My husband's first response was, "Pick up your socks and get over it!" My maternal response was more sympathetic. I talked to our son about the importance of having positive thoughts. We researched the Internet and downloaded a few positive-thinking programs, only to see him continue to spiral downhill. He was confident, attractive, and popular at school, so we were dumbfounded.

If God could create such a magnificent universe, then surely He would provide healing for His creation within it. I was familiar with Revelation 22:2, which tells us that God provided "healing for the nations" from the leaves of the tree of life. The healing leaves are available to all people of all nations, whereas the *fruit*[1] of the tree of life is reserved for the overcomers.[2]

"In the midst of the street of it, and on either side of the river, was there the tree of life, which bare twelve manner of fruits, and yielded her fruit every month: and the leaves of the tree were for the healing of the nations" (Revelation 22:2).

During the same time period, a girlfriend and I met up in Montreal for a few days. A double-degree high school teacher, she shared with me her current side work, which involved healing using energy laws. I was intrigued. Afterward, the long-distance process of our son's healing began. Over the course of one year, we watched a miracle slowly take place before our eyes. Our son learned how to speak a new language, how to develop a new thought process, and how to apply and flow with the laws that are already in place, instead of fighting against them unaware. This was my family's first introduction to energy healing using these laws.

Now, three years later, our son is truly abundant. He creates his reality at will. His abundance does not come on

---

[1] Galatians 5:22–23
[2] Revelation 2:7

account of his human ego but from learning to apply these universal laws to his day-to-day life. Now in his senior year as an engineering major, he lives each day in amazement at what shows up as a result of his new perspective and reality. It is thrilling to see him so high on life yet so well-grounded.

Does God care about all sides of our lives? Many of us Christians feel that God is only interested in the spiritual side of our lives or in that which *affects* the spiritual side. However, the spiritual, mental, and physical planes interpenetrate each other, and according to the hermetic law of correspondence, a situation on one of these levels shows up on the other two.[3] We will come to understand that we have a measure of power over our external world by learning how to tap into our inner world. Therefore, our outer world is a reflection of our inner world. The rules of each universal law are applied the same on all three planes. The higher plane of consciousness will always overcome a lower plane, meaning that a small amount of mental energy will always overcome a larger amount of physical energy.

We enter the physical plane of consciousness when we are born into this world. This is the three-dimensional world around us that we see, smell, touch, taste, and hear. Most people do not move beyond this plane. The human ego thoughts, emotions, and logic rule at this level.

---

[3] Kybalion, 1908. For more information, go to http://lawsoftheuniverse.weebly.com/law-of-corespondance.html.

We enter into the mental plane as we rise in consciousness and faith, and become aware of our greater being, or our soul's divine intelligence, within us. We understand that we have a measure of power over our physical world, and we learn to move beyond our ego thoughts and emotions. We become in tune with our inner guidance system, which includes our conscience, intuition, and "gut feeling."

As we further rise in consciousness and faith, we enter the spiritual plane, where we feel the blessing of God's love, peace, and joy. With it comes the other fruit of the Spirit, namely, compassion, humility, selflessness, and endurance. At this level, we are aware of the promptings of the Holy Spirit, leading us toward truth and love.

The higher our faith or consciousness on the spiritual plane, the less interest we have in creating or focusing on the lower planes. The lower planes will take care of themselves, as we do not attach the negative lower energies to them that would otherwise cause our focus to remain there. I will talk more about this throughout the book.

As you will come to understand, our energy is not confined to our physical bodies. Have you ever *felt* someone watching you from across a crowded room? Have you ever *felt* someone sneaking up on you? Have you ever *felt* someone's sadness? If you have, then what you felt was that person's energy vibration.

One time in the middle of the night, I awoke abruptly and sat up in bed with a dark, heavy feeling of doom and gloom, like nothing I had ever experienced before. I mentally ran through my list of family members to make sure that they were all where they were supposed to be. Our oldest child was with my husband visiting in the Ukraine, and the three other children were safely sleeping in their beds. What on earth was this feeling all about? A few minutes later, my husband called me to announce that he and our son had just been robbed in a Kiev subway, and asked me to cancel the credit cards. Wow, I had felt that negative energy from across the world, from the Ukraine to Canada!

I want to share with you how this book came to be. One afternoon, as I was unpacking boxes in my basement, a young Christian lady's face kept appearing to me, almost to the point of annoyance. I spoke aloud to God, "Please make it obvious to me if you want me to connect with her." In short, she ended up in the next town, in the same building, all alone and in front of me the very next day. How does it get any more obvious than that?

It turns out that this dear young woman was praying that someone would help her in her desperation. Outwardly, she appeared to be confident and happy. Inwardly, she was plagued with fears and anxiety. She burst into tears when I told her of my vision in the basement. Thus began our journey together. I could tell that she, because of her weakened spiritual state, was not yet ready to hear about energy and vibration, so I researched the Scriptures, seeking a biblical language I could use. I knew that these universal laws must be recorded somewhere in the Bible, because of their obvious significance in daily life that even we experienced with our son. As I had expected, all of the laws are in the Bible, so I now have a compilation of Scripture that coincides with each energy law that we worked with.

Since then, I have been drawn to others in similar situations, and the results have been very inspiring. "How come I didn't know about this?" is the common response. Yet some of us are very familiar with most of these Scriptures, but we just tend to *spiritualize* these verses, not realizing that they were meant for all facets of our lives, because we are one being. It was laid upon my heart to record my findings into something accessible for others. I had no idea if this meant an online book or a blog, so I asked God to please make it obvious to me if I was supposed to write a book. Later that afternoon while I was working at my desk, *Balboa Press, A Division of Hay House* came floating across my computer screen in bold letters. Who was I to question now? The process of writing this book began to unfold seamlessly.

I do not believe that God intended us to use these universal laws just to create a meaningful and joyful life on the lower planes. No, I believe He provided these laws as a learning tool on the physical plane to help us understand how to increase our faith in matters that concern the heart and soul as we rise in consciousness.

"I have spoken to you of earthly things and you do not believe; how then will you believe if I speak of heavenly things?" (John 3:12)

Is Jesus suggesting that belief must first begin on the lower earthly plane of consciousness before we can ascend to higher faith into the spiritual plane?

I have talked to a number of fellow Christians and others who seem to have at least one family member who struggles with depression, anxiety, stress, or fear. The spiritual advice that is given to these struggling folks most often is to continue to read, pray, and have faith. This is great advice, but what does it really mean in our practical everyday life, the stresses of which can be overwhelming and all-consuming? How do we actually increase our faith so we stop fearing or stressing? We all know that perfect love casts out fear. If we love God, then why do we still have certain negative thoughts that just bring on more fear, stress, and worry?

I would like to share with you some practical steps you can take in a normal day to increase your faith, to deepen your love, to turn fear into trust, to have power over your negative thoughts, and to actualize what you desire in your reality on all planes, to name a few. Please understand that the focus of this book is not about salvation or redemption.

Rather, it is about tapping into the universal flow that God has provided for our everyday health, healing, and living—the *leaves* on the tree of life, if you will.

As you read this book, you may find that parts of it jump out at you. You might have an "aha" moment as a light bulb goes on. If you feel *light* when reading and the words resonate with you, then that specific message is true for you. However, if you read a sentence or a paragraph that gives you a heavy and uncomfortable feeling, then those words are *not* true for you. Be aware of whether you are reacting emotionally (with the ego) or energetically (with soul intuition, gut feeling, lightness, and heaviness). Try to get a feel for your own energy as you read. Tune out logic, the ways you have always looked at things, and the things you have always believed. Listen to your energy and trust it. Whatever resonates with you energetically will be true for you.

My hope is that my story helps anyone who suffers in silence and wonders why God is allowing this, as well as for anyone who wants to proactively rise to new levels of faith or higher consciousness in order to attract more abundance into life experiences. I have even included a bit of science for any unbelievers. It is my hope that your understanding and application of these universal laws will propel you forward to live abundantly by choice.

Chapter 1

LAW OF VIBRATION

The law of vibration states that, because of our connection with a universal energy force, our thoughts and feelings have the ability to manipulate this vibrating energy force to our liking. [1] Our thoughts and feelings attract a corresponding energy to us. If our thoughts and feelings are negative, then we attract negative experiences. If our feelings are positive, then we attract more positive experiences. The essential message of the law of vibration is that we all have the power to determine our own reality. Through fully and consistently applying this law and shifting our energy accordingly, we can be who we want to be and attract what we want into our reality.

Everything that exists in the universe (whether seen or unseen), when broken down and analyzed in its most basic form, consists of pure energy of vibrating atoms.

---

[1] For more information, visit http://lawsoftheuniverse.weebly.com/law-of-vibration.html.

Newtonian physics held that atoms were of a solid nature.[2] Albert Einstein's world-changing discovery proved that atoms could be broken down and analyzed further, and that the subatomic particles that collectively form the atoms are pure energy. Einstein believed that the energy he had discovered was in the form of particles even though it had an appearance of being solid. Although he was partially correct, his theory differed from that of another noted physicist of that day. Thomas Young believed that energy was not particles at all but, rather, that it existed as a wave form.

The two scientists disagreed over whether subatomic energies were in wave or particle form. Based on these two theories, everything in the universe—the moon, your kitchen sink, a stool, your car, you—can be broken down into its simplest component of vibrating energy. The only difference between the two theories is the rate of speed at which the particles are vibrating. Like vibrations attract each other and will appear as one particular object.

In 1922 a scientist by the name of Niels Bohr suggested that energy can appear in *both* particle and wave form, but never in both forms at the same time.[3] He suggested that

---

[2] For more on this topic, go to http://www.abundance-and-happiness.com/quantum-physics.html.

[3] For more about Bohr, visit http://www.livescience.com/32016-niels-bohr-atomic-theory.html.

energy has the potential to take various forms. In 1927, Bohr and other scientists got together in Brussels to perform an experiment, the famous Copenhagen Interpretation, which proved that subatomic particles could exist either as waves *or* as particles of energy—but not at the same time.[4]

The fact of the matter is that subatomic particles are wave energy. However, when attention is placed on them, they collapse, and particle matter is formed. As observed in the Copenhagen Interpretation, energy took form based on the thoughts and beliefs of the scientist observing it. If he expected to see waves, then he saw waves. If he expected to see particles (i.e., matter), then he saw particles.

What is the conclusion? Whatever thoughts you intensely focus on (wave form) will come into existence (particle form or matter), based on your level of belief. In other words, you see what you believe.

Dr. Joe Dispenza, DC, a researcher specializing in neuroscience, explains it this way: "When you are truly focused on an intention for some future outcome, and if you can make inner thought more real than the outer environment during the process, the brain will not know the difference between the two. Then your body, as the unconscious mind, will begin to experience the new future

---

[4] To read more about the Copenhagen Interpretation, go to http://abyss.uoregon.edu/~js/21st_century_science/lectures/lec15.html.

event in the present moment. You will signal new genes, in new ways, to prepare for this imagined future event."[5]

What does this mean for healing the body of disease or sickness?

Dr. Dispenza states that if you can experience a healing over and over again in the inner world of thoughts and feelings, then healing should, in time, manifest as an outer experience. If you make a *thought* as real as the *experience* in the external environment, then sooner or later you should find evidence in your body and brain. In other words, if you repeatedly mentally rehearse the unknown future with a clear intention and an elevated feeling, then you should experience real neuroplastic changes in your brain and epigenetic changes in your body. This latest research supports the notion that we have a natural ability to change the brain and body by thought alone so that it looks biologically like some future event has already happened.[6]

Based on the foregoing, we can conclude that we attract and become what we send out via our thoughts and beliefs. What if you have negative or fearful thoughts and limiting beliefs? Fortunately, you can begin to overpower these harmful thoughts and beliefs with spoken words and the

---

[5] Joe Dispenza, *You Are the Placebo: Making Your Mind Matter* (London: Hay House UK Limited, 2014).

[6] Ibid.

mind-set that you already are who you want to be. Your language must confirm this new, positive mind-set. The more you speak with positive undertones (even if you do not believe them at first), the sooner your thoughts and brain paths will change. Our subconscious does not know the difference between true and false. It believes what it hears most frequently, which becomes ingrained in the brain paths.[7]

All matter, thoughts, and feelings have their own vibration frequency. Thoughts and feelings of love, peace, and joy have a high vibrating frequency. In contrast, feelings of anger, fear, guilt, apathy, hate, or shame have a low, dense frequency. In other words, your thoughts are inseparably connected to the rest of the universe. As you choose good thoughts, more good thoughts of the same nature will follow, and you will also be in vibration harmony with others who have like thoughts. Your feeling at the present moment dictates your vibration.

The most common unit of measure for vibration frequency is the hertz, which is one vibration cycle per second. A frequency of 460 Hz means that there are 460 cycles of vibration occurring every second. If a frequency is vibrating fast enough, it is emitted as a color of light. If we wanted to convert sound to light, we would simply

---

[7] Dr. Shad Helmstetter, What to Say When You Talk to Yourself, Pocket Books, Simon & Schuster, 1982

raise the sound's frequency forty octaves. This results in a vibration in the trillions of cycles per second. If a pianist could press a key far above the eighty-eight keys that exist on a piano, that key would produce light. A chord of light could be created in the same way as a chord of sound. It would be seen as colors of light because it would be moving at the speed of light. Hence Einstein's theory of relativity, where energy is related to matter and the speed of light, resulting in his famous equation $E = mc^2$.[8]

How does this relate to us and our thoughts? What would it mean to you if you could increase your level of consciousness or vibration frequency so as to *create* your world instead of *reacting* to it, to go from depression to liberation, from fear to love, from misery to joy, from guilt to trust, from lack to abundance? This all begins with a thought reinforced with a belief.

This vibration law is working throughout the universe all the time, whether we understand it or not. Look around you and within you to see what it is you are attracting into your world. In practical terms, this law is not about attracting what you *want* but about attracting what you *are*. Therefore, if you would like something different from what you have around you in your physical world to show up,

---

[8] For more on this, see https://hiddenlighthouse.wordpress.com/category/law-of-vibration/.

then you must adjust your mental energy to match what you want to attract.

Applying this law means to *desire, visualize,* and *feel* what it is you want to attract into your life *as if you have already received it*. Like energy will attract the same energy.

Following is an example of how to apply this law in a practical situation. After searching out various universities, our second son felt the *lightest* about attending the highly regarded engineering program at McGill University in Montreal, even though he had submitted his application four months past the deadline. One day in mid-July, he put his arm around me and said with his usual charm and delight, "Mom, did you know that I am going to McGill?"

I was thrilled and asked, "You received their letter of acceptance?"

He said, "No, not yet, but I will." He had a *knowing*. He had set his intention, familiarized himself with the McGill website, and visualized himself walking down the school hallway and playing the grand piano in the atrium. In his mind, he was already going there. He had sent out the question into the unknown, "What would it take for me to get accepted into McGill?" He was certainly qualified, but so were hundreds of other students on the waiting list. Then, he left it with God, knowing that it was taken care of because it felt so right and light. And it was. He received the acceptance letter a few weeks later.

We all have a unique path and purpose in life. If our requests can contribute to God's purpose for our lives, then it will be granted in support of our freewill choices and according to our faith. If a choice we make is not right for us overall, then we will hit resistance, time and time again. We will know that we are on the right path if there is flow and space.

To be clear, applying the law of vibration on the physical plane is not about slacking in life and making demands. It is more about attracting what is right for you, getting clear direction, and then acting on inspiration, trust, and faith. It may mean applying to a school, picking up a pen and paper, choosing the right partner, making a phone call, applying for the right job, or something else. It is not about sitting on a couch and making demands with an attitude of entitlement. In fact, the higher our level of consciousness, the less our ego is involved.

Law of Faith

"Now faith is the substance of things hoped for, the evidence of things not seen" (Hebrews 11:1).

Ultimate faith is a high-vibrating energy partnered with other fruit of the Spirit, such as love, peace, joy, serenity, compassion, appreciation, and humility. Without faith or belief, perpetual abundance is unachievable on all planes.

I will talk more about this in the section on the law of abundance.

How does faith relate to the law of vibration? Let us start at the beginning.

"And God said, Let us make man in our image, after our likeness" (Genesis 1:26).

God willed creation into being through word and thought. He gave that same power to humanity. We have the power to will our own reality into being through our thoughts and through the spoken word, but *only* as much as our faith or belief will allow.

Do you think your thoughts are private? They are not. Our thoughts emit an energy that is sent out to the universe (God).

Hebrews 4:12 reads, "For the word of God is quick ... and is a discerner of the thoughts and intents of the heart."

Be extra careful with what you say after speaking the phrase *I am*, such as, "I am sad," "I am mad," or "I am poor," because you are empowering those words. Whenever you say "I am," add the word that you wish to be. "I am strong"; "I am creative"; "I am full of life"; "I am abundant"; "I am loved"; "I am happy"; etc.

"Let the weak say, I am strong" (Joel 3:10).

Our spoken words and thoughts culminate in belief, which then solidifies into our reality. Jesus confirms this power of belief. He said, "Therefore I say unto you, What things soever ye desire, when ye pray, believe that ye receive them, and ye shall have them" (Mark 11:24).

This magical and powerful verse is the secret to bringing into being what you desire (manifestation) on all planes. These words describe the law of vibration (attraction) in its entirety. If we can truly comprehend what Jesus is saying here, then we know that *how* we ask or pray is critical. When we pray to God, He receives far more from us than just our words. The level of faith or belief that radiates from us is more powerful than any words we can utter. "But without faith it is impossible to please him: for he that cometh to God must believe that he is, and that he is a rewarder of them that diligently seek him." (Hebrews 11:6)

If we make a petition to God but do not really believe that He is, that He can, or that He will, then our prayer will be ineffectual.

In Mark 11:23, Jesus says, "For verily I say unto you, That whosoever shall say unto this mountain, Be thou removed, and be thou cast into the sea; and shall not doubt in his heart, but shall believe that those things which he saith shall come to pass; he shall have whatsoever he saith."

These words of Jesus are not just a figure of speech to illustrate his point. If we truly have the same level of faith that Jesus had, then we would believe that the mountain could be moved, and so it would be, according to our faith. It is difficult for the human mind to even comprehend this.

How do we pray effectively? Jesus prayed in many different ways. However, I love how he prayed before some of the more profound miracles took place. He thanked God for the miracle *before* it even happened! We read of Jesus raising Lazarus from the dead in John 11. He did not say, "Father, please raise Lazarus from the dead." Instead, he prayed, "Father, I thank thee that thou hast heard me." This is concerning Lazarus, as if the miracle had already taken place. Jesus had faith that Lazarus would rise, and so Lazarus rose. Belief must come before the miracle. The real miracle here was not that Lazarus *rose* from the dead. The real miracle was that Jesus *believed* that Lazarus would rise from the dead.

Another example of this type of prayer is when Jesus fed the four thousand men, beside women and children, with only seven loaves of bread and a few fishes (as recounted in Matthew 15). Again, Jesus, never doubting, gave thanks to God for the food that was going to feed the multitude *before* this miracle took place. And so it was. Everyone was fed and satisfied. In fact, there were seven baskets of food left over. If Jesus had said, "This is not enough food," then the loaves and fishes would not have been enough.

We read in 2 Kings 4 of the widow woman who was going to lose her two sons to her late husband's creditor. All she had left of monetary value in her house was a small pot of oil. Elisha, a man of God, told her to go and gather jars from the neighbors to pour the oil into. We do not know how many the widow gathered and poured oil into, but we do know that each jar was filled. The oil increased to fill each jar and then it stopped when the jars stopped. She gathered as many jars as she believed would be filled. I believe that if she had gathered more jars, then there would have been more oil. If she had gathered fewer jars, then there would have been less oil. This is a beautiful picture of how faith works. God responds to our requests based on what our faith will allow, nothing more and nothing less.

I thought of Moses and the great miracles that God performed for the Israelites. God performed the miracles, but Moses's belief came first. Prior to the manifestation of the two miracles below, Moses acted first in faith by stretching or raising his hand as God requested, which signified his belief.

- Exodus 14:21: "And Moses stretched out his hand over the sea; and the Lord caused the sea to go back by a strong east wind all that night, and made the sea dry land, and the waters were divided."
- Exodus 17:11: "And it came to pass, when Moses held up his hand, that Israel prevailed: and when he let down his hand, Amalek prevailed."

All that is required for the impossible to occur is belief on our part. Our words and actions signify our faith. God takes care of the rest. As is said in Luke 1:37, "For with God nothing shall be impossible."

In John 2, we read of there being no wine at a marriage supper. Jesus asked the servants to fill six stone pots with water (approximately twenty gallons each). They not only filled the pots, but filled them to the brim. Jesus then asked them to draw out from the water pots and give what they drew to the governor of the feast. So they did. Then a miracle took place.

John 2:9–10 reads, "When the ruler of the feast had tasted the water that was made wine, and knew not whence it was: (but the servants which drew the water knew;) the governor of the feast called the bridegroom, And saith unto him, Every man at the beginning doth set forth good wine; and when men have well drunk, then that which is worse: but thou hast kept the good wine until now."

This miracle of water being changed to wine took place *after* the servants acted in faith by drawing out from the water pots. Their obedient action signified their belief, and their faith contributed to this great miracle.

If believing is what is required, then can I receive anything at all that I ask for on this physical plane as long as I believe on the mental plane that it will be mine? In Psalms 106, we are told that the Israelites tempted God in the desert by their request. Psalms 106:15 reads, "He gave them their request; but sent leanness into their soul."

There was another time when Moses performed an action that signified his faith; however, it was not in accordance to the will of God. God asked Moses to take the rod (not to use it) and *speak* to the rock so it would yield water for the thirsty nation. Instead, Moses struck the rod twice on the rock in anger and then lectured the nation with a bitter heart. He then overmagnified his own partnership with God when he said, "Hear now, you rebels! Must *we* bring water for you out of this rock?"

Numbers 20:11: "And Moses lifted up his hand, and with his rod he smote the rock twice: and the water came out abundantly, and the congregation drank, and their beasts also."

In spite of Moses's disobedience, God still honored his faith. Water came out of the rock abundantly. However, Moses's actions brought leanness to his soul. After forty years of leading the people toward the Promised Land, Moses was only permitted to view it from a distance and was not permitted to enter. He died and was buried this side of the border.

Therefore, it is always wise to keep the ego in check when making our requests to God and acting in faith. Just because we ask and receive in faith does not mean that our request is the right thing for us overall and will benefit our soul. Are we asking for something from a place of ego or from soul inspiration?

The motive of our request is important. It is always wise to ask for something that will help fulfill your life's purpose. Alternatively, you can always ask God *what* you should ask for; wait for clarity to come; and then follow with what feels right. Alternatively, you can never go wrong by asking for divine wisdom.

James 1:5 reads, "If any of you lack wisdom, let him ask of God, that giveth to all men liberally, and upbraideth not; and it shall be given him."

Jesus reminds us to ask our requests in His name so that God can be glorified in Him. He says in John 14:12–14, "Verily, verily, I say unto you, He that believeth on me, the works that I do shall he do also; and greater works than these shall he do; because I go unto my Father. And whatsoever ye shall ask in my name, that will I do, that the Father may be glorified in the Son. If ye shall ask any thing in my name, I will do it."

When we see that our petition has been granted, it is important that we give God the credit, the thanks, and the glory. Then it becomes a positive cycle. The more thanks and glory we give to God, the more we will receive and the stronger our faith becomes. Even more powerful is giving thanks and glory to God for what you are asking for, as if you have already received it.

How do I know if I have the right amount of faith when I pray? You will know your faith is strong when you have a *knowing* that your petition to God is taken care of. You will get on with your day, no longer burdened with what you left with Him, and you will not feel the need to ask for the same thing again and again. If you leave a burden with God and yet continue to fret about it all day, then you have not left it with Him at all.

Chapter 2

APPLICATION OF THE LAW OF FAITH

I understand that belief must come before I receive what I am requesting, but how do I increase my faith so I truly believe?

Gratitude

Expressing gratitude and appreciation to God for *all* things is the quickest and most effective way to increase your faith (vibration). You will immediately feel a shift of energy, a "lighter" feeling, even as you say the words of thanks.

- "In *every thing give thanks*: for this is the will of God in Christ Jesus concerning you" (1 Thessalonians 5:18).
- "*Giving thanks always for all things unto God*" (Ephesians 5:20).

What if you were to talk to God verbally and thank Him throughout the day, not just morning and night? How about thanking Him for another new beautiful day wherein you can praise and worship Him? Or, perhaps, thank Him for what you are enjoying at the moment—friendship, family, fellowship, a sunset, nature, etc. Example: "Thank You so much for sharing this beautiful sunset with me." I find it very helpful to speak aloud to God, because our ego thoughts consume us most of the day, but the spoken word overpowers these thoughts.

I love this quotation: "Gratitude unlocks the fullness of life. It turns what we have into enough and more. It turns denial into acceptance, chaos into order, and confusion to clarity. It can turn a meal into a feast, a house into a home, a stranger into a friend. Gratitude makes sense of our past, brings peace for today and creates a vision for tomorrow."[1] It illustrates the benefits of a thankful heart and mind.

You will know that you have moved on from an experience in your past when you can truly give thanks for it. You will have used that experience as a boost to propel you forward in life instead of using it as justification for living a life of misery.

Express gratitude for, and to, others in your life. Gratitude affects all areas of your life, including your

---

[1] Melody Beattie, *The Language of Letting Go* (Center City, MN: Hazelden, 1990), 218.

relationships with people at work, your marriage, your relationship with your children, and your friendships. You become a more positive person, more productive, and a higher achiever, and people want to be around you. People love to be appreciated. In fact, my guess is that your spouse, child, friend, or coworker would go out of his or her way to please you more if you displayed gratitude. Gratitude automatically increases your vibration thereby affecting the energy of those around you in a positive way. Everyone wins. When you live in the state of gratitude, you rise higher in faith, so more goodness will be attracted back to you in all areas of your life. If you feel that you have nothing to be grateful for, then your spoken words of thankfulness will slowly begin to override any ungrateful feelings.

Exercise: Whenever you have a quiet moment in your day at the office or on your evening walk, speak verbal words of gratitude to God. Try to do this at least three times every day.

Inner-Guidance Team

Every person on earth has an infinite being, or soul, within. This soul is the connection to divine intelligence, which knows all things about us and all things around us. In contrast, our physical ego (human nature) is temporal and can only reference what we have learned from past experience and the knowledge we have gained from the physical three-dimensional world around us.

Conscience

Our conscience is guidance from our soul and is our moral searchlight given to us at birth by God. Proverbs 20:27 reads, "The spirit of man is the candle of the Lord, searching all the inward parts of the belly."

Our conscience is the voice of our inner being, or soul, which knows all of the things that are best for us.

Our soul, or greater being, is naturally attracted to the divine. I believe that if everyone followed their soul guidance led by our divine team, then this would lead them to their life's purpose. However, too often the conscience is undermined by the ego. In fact, many people tune out the voice of their conscience altogether and are completely led by their ego (human nature).

Our Divine Team

God speaks to our soul, and His words are communicated to us through our conscience (gut feeling and intuition). You will know which way to move forward by which way feels "lighter" or feels intuitively right. Your inner being will not guide you to something that feels heavy or dark.

However, your ego has its own agenda, so it might rebel when you try to follow your conscience. It may send logic or self-condemnation your way to try to get you to revert to your default position—the way you have always done things or your old thought patterns.

One fellow Christian said to me, "I don't know if I can trust my conscience." Your conscience is your soul's guidance, so you can trust it if you are sensitive to it. If we repeatedly choose not to adhere to our conscience, then it can become seared (dulled) and we will no longer feel the promptings of it. Our conscience is the conduit God uses to speak to us. There is a hymn that says, "Speak to my soul, Lord Jesus. Speak now in tender tones." To hear the tender whispers, we need to be still and tune in to our energy, not to our emotions.

Once you learn the difference between the two guidance systems (soul vs. ego), then you will learn not to doubt your conscience. If you follow your conscience, you will know flow, an elevated state of being, freedom, and liberty, and doors will open for you on all planes. Your conscience will lead you to what feels right and light, and you will have a *knowing* that all is going to be okay. Follow your knowing, no matter how big or trivial the situation you are facing is.

Here is an example of a time when I had a *knowing* that all was well in spite of all signs pointing to potential crisis. About three days before my husband and I left home in

Canada for Europe, my passport went missing. I remember taking it out and securing it in a hotel room drawer in another city a few weeks before. The interesting thing was that I had a strange calm because I had this knowing feeling deep down that all was still well. Logic told me that my passport was gone and that I would not be going to Europe anytime soon. Sure enough, the lost passport was found. I soon began to trust my *knowing* radar.

Our conscience serves us on all levels of consciousness. Our inner being wants to guide us throughout our everyday life in all things, large and small, spiritual or physical. It knows what is best for us on all levels.

Hosea wrote in the second chapter of his book about God hedging up a person's way with two walls of thorn bushes and providing an unrestricted path in the middle. If a person kept between the thorn hedges, then there would be flow and space in her journey. As soon as she turned to the right or left, there would be pain and suffering, or blockages. Hosea 2:6 reads, "Therefore, behold, I will hedge up thy way with thorns, and make a wall."

We feel resistance when we turn away from our soul guidance and let our ego dominate. God hedges up our way with thorns to guide us to our purpose. When we are on the right course, everything materializes with relative ease. You will know that you are following your soul's guidance, or conscience, when there is flow in your path.

If you are constantly hitting thorns and roadblocks, then you will know that you are not following your conscience. During times like these, ask God to speak to your soul. His guidance will always feel light and will create flow.

What voice are you listening to? Have you ever gone ahead with a decision even though your gut feeling told you not to? Perhaps your decision sounded like fun, or perhaps it made logical sense, so why would you be having this heavy feeling? How did the situation turn out? Did you end up hitting thorns? Do you ignore this heavy feeling or tune it out by keeping active and busy? Our ego certainly knows how to overpower our conscience to the point that we no longer tune in.

Our Creator has made provision to help revive our conscience and restore it to its rightful place: through our faith in Jesus. Hebrews 9:14 reads, "How much more shall the blood of Christ, who through the eternal Spirit offered himself without spot to God, purge your conscience from dead works to serve the living God?"

As our faith increases, we are given the gift of the Holy Spirit to guide us back on course and our conscience is refreshed and restored. As we learn to follow our conscience, it will lead us to greater faith.

Sometimes we might get confused as to whether it is our conscience or ego that is speaking. Perhaps, we might have feelings of self-condemnation ("I told you so"; "I am not good enough"; "I will never make it"; "I failed again"; "I am not a good Christian"; "I can't do it"). I believe this is not the voice of our conscience but, rather, the voice of our ego. Our conscience is guided by our greater being, which is divine, so it will never condemn us. Jesus did not come to the world to condemn us; He came to save the world. John 3:17 reads, "For God sent not his Son into the world to condemn the world; but that the world through him might be saved."

A young Christian man who ignored his conscience went out drinking with his buddies on a Saturday night. The next morning, he heard a voice in his head telling him that he had failed again and that there was no point in going to church that morning because of what he had done the night before. Is this the condemning voice of his ego or the voice of his conscience? His conscience would have told him to get out of bed and go to a place where he might be inspired. His ego would tell him that he has failed again, so what is the point in going to church? If he had listened to his conscience the first time, then he would not have had to wrestle with self-condemnation after the fact of a night of drinking.

Paul says in Romans 14:22, "Hast thou faith? have it to thyself before God. Happy is he that condemneth not himself in that thing which he alloweth."

Again, it is a good idea to listen to our conscience the first time. Then, we do not have to wrestle with the self-condemnation of our ego, which comes with ignoring the voice of our inner being. Your conscience will offer you guidance. It always knows what is best for you, but it will not condemn you.

Our conscience will guide us through life as choices come up. If we are in tune, it will guide us toward safe and right choices for us. If we make a choice based solely on head logic or emotion and find ourselves in an undesirable situation, then our conscience will always provide an out or another option. It is a matter of tuning in and checking which way is out; it will always feel the lightest. The right way out of a situation will give you a sense of relief.

Paul says in 1 Corinthians 10:13, "There hath no temptation taken you but such as is common to man: but God is faithful, who will not suffer you to be tempted above that ye are able; *but will with the temptation also make a way to escape, that ye may be able to bear it*".

How do I know if it is my conscience or my emotionally driven ego that is guiding me? Our conscience has no emotion, and guides us forward through feelings of lightness and rightness (gut feeling and intuition). Our ego is driving us if we make a decision coming from a place of emotion, such as panic about money, fear about losing someone or something, anger at our children or mother-in-law, etc. An ego question might be, "What's in it for me?" In contrast, our conscience will ask, "How can I serve today?"

I was going to add the word *conviction* as something that is a part of our inner guidance system, but I could not even find the word in the Bible to reference it. We tend to use that word in the context of, "I was moved with conviction to …" Does this suggest that we were moved by guilt and not by love? Feelings of guilt are in the same low-vibration category as fear. We do not read of Jesus ever using the word *conviction*. He came to give us light, liberty, and freedom from guilt, not to convict or condemn us. Again, is feeling "convicted" a result of self-condemnation from the ego? Or perhaps this is just a negative word choice we use when what we really mean is we were *moved by our conscience*. How do we know the difference? If your *conviction* makes you feel heavy or burdened, then more than likely it is self-condemnation of the ego. When you follow your conscience, it will always feel right and light.

There were many who came to Jesus with a heavy burden of sin. He released them from their sin and said, "Go and sin no more." These people left lighter than when they came. Our conscience will always spur us on to do the right thing. It might be wise to look inward and see what convictions or deep-rooted beliefs we have that are not from the doctrine of Jesus, such as religious traditions or beliefs from our childhood that cause us to remain stuck.

Sometimes we can become so stuck in our ways that these beliefs become attachments to the earth like anything else we would covet, and hinders the freedom of the Holy Spirit. Perhaps we need to let go of or relax some of the old rooted beliefs to give room and liberty for the Holy Spirit to show us something greater and allow it to bring us up to the next level of faith.

Here is a biblical example of the soul-ego forces at play. Pontius Pilate, the Roman Governor of Judea, had the power to put Jesus on the cross or to release him. John 19:12 reads, *"And from thenceforth Pilate sought to release him: but the Jews cried out, saying, If thou let this man go, thou art not Caesar's friend: whosoever maketh himself a king speaketh against Caesar"*.

Luke 23:4 reads, "Then said Pilate to the chief priests and to the people, *I find no fault in this man*".

Pilate's soul guidance (conscience) told him that Jesus was an innocent man. However, Pilate allowed his ego to overrule his conscience. He chose to please the people and put Jesus on the cross.

Judas Iscariot was also governed by his ego when he sold Jesus for thirty pieces of silver to be crucified (see Matthew 27). When he realized the seriousness of what he had done, he wrestled with self-condemnation and ended his own life. If he had been in tune with his inner guidance, then he would have been led back to Jesus in repentance so he could know forgiveness.

Your conscience is speaking when you have an inner *knowing*, even if it may not make logical sense. The more you tune in and follow the lightness of your own inner energy, the more goodness will flow into your everyday life.

I am sure that we have all experienced a *gut feeling* at some time in our lives. We had a *knowing*, yet probably did not understand at the time that it was soul guidance. I remember planning for a family trip to Thailand in December 2004. We were deciding whether to fly to Chiang Mai from Koh Samui (via Bangkok) or from Phuket (which was a direct flight). Being that it meant one less flight for the six of us, I rooted for the latter. My husband insisted that he did not have a good feeling about Phuket, so we ended up going to Koh Samui. As it turned out, we were having breakfast on the morning of December 26, 2004, in a Koh Samui resort when we learned that Phuket had just been hit by a tsunami. Over two hundred thousand people were killed on that coast that day. Learn to trust your *gut feeling* or *knowing*. I am so thankful that my husband trusted his.

If you follow your lightness in everyday little things one day at a time, it will lead you to your greater purpose. We know we are following our lightness / soul guidance when our world becomes brighter and we feel various degrees of

Application of the Law of Faith

joy akin to a light helium feeling. Divine joy of the soul is a higher-elevated feeling than emotional happiness.

Do your closest friends and family know what is best for you? As much as they may know and love you, they do not know what is true and right for the real you. Your ego does not even know what is true for you. When making life choices, it is okay to ask others for opinions and suggestions, but always choose what feels the lightest. Be careful about making decisions based on pure logic when it concerns your life goals.

Does God care about all the details of your life such as your relationships, what business you start, what school you put your kids into, your health, your financial situation, etc.? Whatever you believe will be true for you. If you believe He cares and invite Him into your day, then He will be involved in the details of your life according to your faith. In Matthew 6:30, Jesus says, "Wherefore, if God so clothe the grass of the field, which to day is, and to morrow is cast into the oven, shall he not much more clothe you, O ye of little faith?"

If God cares about the grass of the field that is here today and gone tomorrow, then how much more He must care about the details of our lives. In fact, I believe He makes it His business once faith becomes involved. He is delighted when we include Him throughout our day, just as a tender parent is happy to be involved with all aspects of his child's life. God cares about and responds to our faith meter concerning the details of our lives because He understands that our outer world is a reflection of our inner world and that we are one being.

We can move on to greater faith and be brought into His love and peace when we learn to trust the provision and care of God on the lower physical and mental planes of consciousness.

I believe we are meant to live our life with joy. However, joy is not just handed over to us. We go through a lot of lower-level experiences where we learn how to attain it. Sometimes we might have to hit rock bottom with an experience before we realize that the answers are within us. If we can tune in to our inner guidance and follow it every day, then we will learn to flow through these tough experiences.

If the divine is guiding our conscience, then who or what is controlling the ego? Our ego is very much influenced by three things: the *world* or the environment around us, our own desires and the weaknesses of our *flesh*, and the low energies we take on, including the deceitful wiles of *Satan*.

First John 2:16 reads, "For all that is in the *world*, the lust of the *flesh*, and the lust of the eyes, and the pride of life, is not of the Father, but is of the world."

Paul says in Ephesians 6:11, "Put on the whole armour of God, that ye may be able to stand against the *wiles of the devil.*"

Our ego is necessary and useful if used for good as intended by our Creator. It is the vehicle God uses to fulfill our soul's purpose. He can use our ego talents and natural gifts for our good and also for the good of others. Our ego is the accumulation of a lifetime's worth of experiences, emotions, baggage, trauma, issues, hopes, and inspirations all in one package. It processes information for everyday living. Just because a thought comes into our head does not mean that we have to believe it. Considering that every thought we have gets filtered through our ego, it is our job to weigh each of our thoughts and decide whether or not we want to accept them. Our conscience will help us with this. If a thought feels light and resonates with us, then it is safe to accept.

The ego is subject to human temptations. Adam and Eve could have been made perfect without temptation of the ego if they had not sinned in the garden. However, they wanted to be like gods and to know good *and* evil, so they ate from the tree that God asked them not to eat from. We do not need to feel like they did us a disservice as a result of their sin, because we know that God appreciates the redeemed person who has faith (with ego in check) over the innocent person who could have been made perfect. I

Application of the Law of Faith

like the picture of this that a California fruit farmer gave me one time. He said that the sweetest fruit is produced when a cultivated fruit plant is grafted onto wild rootstock. When faith is grafted onto our ego, it produces a richer, sweeter, and more meaningful existence.

God sends the extra help and guidance of His *Holy Spirit* to His believing people as a guide and Comforter.

The apostle Paul says in Ephesians 1:12-13, "That we should be to the praise of his glory, who first trusted in Christ. In whom ye also trusted, after that ye heard the word of truth, the gospel of your salvation: *in whom also after that ye believed, ye were sealed with that Holy Spirit of promise.*"

In John 14:16–18, Jesus says, "And I will pray the Father, and he shall give you another Comforter, that he may abide with you for ever; Even the Spirit of truth; whom the world cannot receive, because it seeth him not, neither knoweth him: but ye know him; for he dwelleth with you, and shall be in you. I will not leave you comfortless: I will come to you."

There are times in my own life when I feel that the presence of the Holy Spirit is more prevalent than at other times, which probably has more to do with my own level of faith or consciousness at that particular time. At these times, the Holy Spirit feels like a cloud descending, completely enveloping me in ultimate comfort, love, and peace. This is most prevalent during times of communion when a number of people are gathered in harmony and unity in collective high faith, which seems to invite the Holy Spirit in its fullness. The Holy Spirit is sent by God to the believers at His discretion to guide us into all truth.

Jesus says in John 16:13, "Howbeit when He, the Spirit of Truth, is come, He will guide you into all truth; for He shall not speak from Himself, but whatsoever He shall hear, that shall He speak; and He will show you things to come."

Who else is part of our divine team in addition to God the Father, Jesus the Son, and the Holy Spirit? *Angels* are also part of the team because they are our helpers and ministering spirits, guiding us to light. The Bible mentions numerous types of angels, such as cherubim, seraphim, thrones, dominions, powers, principalities, and archangels, all serving different purposes.

God has provided us with these angelic helpers in this life as part of our divine team. I like to think that each person on the planet has been assigned at least one guardian angel. These angels help guide us to our life's purpose.

Jesus says in Matthew 18:10, "Take heed that ye despise not one of these little ones; for I say unto you, That in heaven *their* angels do always behold the face of my Father which is in heaven."

Psalms 91:11 reads, "For he shall give his angels charge over thee, to keep thee in all thy ways."

I believe that angels are ascending and descending all around us. Some of us have had our own angel experiences, which confirms their existence to us. We might get a quick glimpse of one nearby when we see a white flash out of the corner of our eye. However, normally we cannot see angels because they operate at a much higher vibration frequency than we do. Having said this, they can descend to a lower level of consciousness and appear in human form to fulfill a specific purpose.

Hebrews 13:2 reads, "Be not forgetful to entertain strangers: for thereby some have entertained angels unawares."

A young, loving mother I know very well had slipped out the front door of her house one day to run around to the back to retrieve something quickly, leaving her two-year-old toddler playing with his toys in the living room. All in the span of two or three minutes, the toddler reached up, unlocked and opened the door, and then walked out onto the busy street's sidewalk looking for his mom. Then a man appeared, picked up the toddler, and put him back inside the house. The man waited there outside the door for the mother to appear, which she did a few seconds later. This kind and gentle man appeared at the right time, and then he was suddenly gone. Was this man an angel?

Is it okay to ask God to send His angels to our assistance or to the assistance of someone else? I believe that if we ask, our request will be granted according to our faith. God dispatches His angels according to His will.

I had my two-year-old grandbaby for the night. It went fairly well getting him settled for the night, until he awoke in the early hours of the morning screaming for his mother. Nothing would calm him. Finally, after an hour of his relentless crying, I was at my wits' end, so I asked God to send His angels to help settle the child. The response was immediate. There was a calm that came into the room that I cannot explain even to this day. My grandbaby stopped crying immediately and looked around wide-eyed. He then closed his eyes and went to sleep. I left my little man then, knowing that he would be taken care of. He slept soundly for the rest of the night. I know my request was granted because I *believed* that help would come.

The best way we can thank the angels for their help is *to thank God* for the gift of His angels. Payment to them is giving God the credit and glory for their help. We are reminded in the book of Revelation that angels are not to be worshipped. John was reprimanded at least twice for falling down and worshipping an angel. Angels are fellow servants and are here to fulfill a purpose, just as we are.

Revelation 22:8–9 reads, "And I John saw these things, and heard them. And when I had heard and seen, I fell down to worship before the feet of the angel which shewed me these things. Then saith he unto me, See thou do it not: for I am thy fellow servant, and of thy brethren the prophets, and of them which keep the sayings of this book: worship God."

Angels sent from God will always guide you toward a higher consciousness and greater love. Remember to follow the inner guidance that feels light. With lightness comes clarity and direction. God's angels will never guide you toward something that feels heavy and dark. You will always be right if you follow your peace.

Romans 14:19 reads, "Let us therefore follow after the things which make for peace."

Prayer and Meditation

The more we practice prayer and meditation, the more we will understand that this is a *state of being* rather than something we physically do only morning and night by our bedside. It is a matter of being present and aware, seeing God in all things, thinking about and speaking to Him throughout the day, and being in tune with our inner guidance.

God speaks to us and inspirations come when we are in the *present moment*, not when our minds are wandering to the conversation we had yesterday, to what we have to do today, or to potential future happenings. The body seems to want to anticipate the next moment, and then the moment after, based on past experiences. When you are fully in the present moment, you are not thinking about old, negative brain-circuit programs from the past, because you are now *being*. New inspirations come when we are in the present moment.

Be present, not only in your prayer life but also throughout your day. My husband often affirmed this concept of being present to our children. He would say, "Wherever you are, *be there!*" In other words, be there in the moment in mind as well as in body. Do not wish you were somewhere else. The kids understood that headsets or earbuds were not to be used during family time. Tuning out was not permitted in the car on the way to school or when sitting around the table. Actually, I found that the drive to and from school was a wonderful time to communicate with my kids. They were not threatened by eye contact, so they somehow felt free to share what they would not normally share around the kitchen table.

It is only when we are in this state of being present that we are available on all levels to God and to those around us. God calls Himself "I Am," signifying that He is very present, not "I was" or "I will be." We are in communion with Him when we, also, are in that *I Am* present state.

Exodus 3:14 reads, "And God said unto Moses, I Am That I Am: and he said, Thus shalt thou say unto the children of Israel, I Am hath sent me unto you."

Application of the Law of Faith

How do we get into the present moment of prayer and meditation when we have so much mind traffic? Being conscious of each breath you take helps you be present, because it takes your focus off your thoughts. Deepen your breath, understanding that each breath is a gift of life from our Creator. As you seek to get into the present moment, where God is, thoughts will come to you about the past or about what you have to do that day (and so forth). Let these thoughts come and observe them float by like a cloud, but hold no emotional attachment to them. When we try to shoo these thoughts away, we are actually attaching emotion, positive or negative, to them, which will only attract more of the same energy and thoughts. Understand that it is just beyond these thoughts where you come into the present moment, which is where you can connect to the mind of our Creator. It is not very far away. So allow the thoughts to float by as they come. Refocus on your breath, and then repeat the process. By constantly going back to your breathing, you are gradually breaking the cycle of mind traffic. Pretty soon, the unwanted thoughts will have less amplitude and hold less power. You know you are getting close when you become neutral and no longer react to the thoughts in your head.

When you finally get to that *sweet spot* just beyond your thoughts, you might feel an expansion upward and outward. You may no longer be aware of your body as you become almost pure consciousness. Your body goes from matter to liberation of energy and from particle to wave. You will now be in a space of *being*, where you can now be in communion with our Creator.

Try to end your day in this spirit of prayer. As Paul says in Ephesians 4:26, "Let not the sun go down upon your wrath."

There is a good reason why we should not go to bed angry or upset. Use wisely the interval preceding sleep. The sensation that dominates the mind of a person as he or she falls asleep may be sealed into the subconscious.

Job 33:15–16 reads, "In a dream, in a vision of the night, when deep sleep falleth upon men, in slumberings upon the bed; Then he openeth the ears of men, and sealeth their instruction."

This controlled waking dream state just before sleep is the most critical time of the day to mentally actualize what it is we prayerfully desire. If we spend this critical time with worry, fears, or anger, then such things may be sealed in our subconscious as we go into a deep sleep. If we find ourselves lying awake stressed and worried, like some of us mothers do, this might be a good time to whisper words of gratitude to God, or to speak positive words of "I am …" This will shift your negative energy immediately.

Application of the Law of Faith

Here is another verse in Matthew's Gospel that reinforces the power of this belief: "And all things, whatsoever ye shall ask in prayer, believing, ye shall receive" (Matthew 21:22).

Another type of prayer is to ask God open-ended questions, which leaves open the door for His possibly giving us something far greater than what we could even think of asking for.

Examples of open-ended prayers or meditation are as follows:

- "Dear Father, what do I need to learn from this experience that I am not getting?"
- "What would it take to change this situation?"
- "What would it take to [whatever you desire to create]?"
- "What is really possible here that I haven't yet considered?"
- "What can I add to my life today that will generate meaning and abundance now and in the future?"
- "What else is possible?"
- "What would it take to increase my faith?"
- "What would it take for me to learn patience?"

Try to stay away from asking God for specific outcomes for situations, because you are then setting limitations on what He can do for you. Be patient after asking. God lives in one eternal now. There is no past or present for Him. However, we are temporal beings who live in the context of time. When you pray in faith, God immediately gives you what you prayed for—in the spiritual plane. However, in the physical world, due to a number of factors, it may take time for the answer to manifest itself. God answers prayers, and He will answer your specific prayer in line with His Word, but it is your faith that can bring the answer out of the spiritual plane and into the physical plane. How many times in the Bible does Jesus say to someone, "According to your faith"? Jesus referred to people's faith constantly even though it was God's power that healed them. He always credited their faith as being the catalyst for the reason the miracle happened.

In Daniel 10, Daniel prayed the same prayer for his people and country for twenty-one days, seemingly without a response from God. Then an angel appeared to him. Daniel 10:12–13 reads as follows:

> Then said he unto me, Fear not, Daniel: for from the first day that thou didst set thine heart to understand, and to chasten thyself before thy God, thy words were heard, and I am come for thy words. But the prince of the kingdom of Persia withstood me one and twenty days: but, lo, Michael, one of the chief

> princes, came to help me; and I remained there with the kings of Persia.

Perhaps Daniel thought his prayer was not heard by God when, in fact, God was working on Daniel's behalf in the background for the twenty-one days he prayed the prayer. When you pray, have faith that God has heard, has answered, and is working on your request for you in the background. It is your faith that can bring about the manifestation of that prayer.

Find time in your day to be alone with your Creator. Be still, and allow Him to download the fruit of the Spirit into your life. As Psalms 46:10 says, "Be still, and know that I am God:"

It is also important to remember others in your prayers. I believe that when I pray for someone, a thought of God passes through that person's mind at that very moment, no matter what he or she is doing. If you believe that, then it is so. If you do not believe it, then it is not so. Try to remember that the person you pray for also has a free will, so it might be wise to be careful about crossing that line in your prayer. Example: It might be ineffective to pray that Sally would end her relationship with Jack because that would be crossing both their free wills. Alternatively, you can never go wrong by asking God to remember and touch Sally's heart or soul if you have a concern for her.

The more you do this while believing, the more her heart will be touched by God, and the greater chance that she will respond to the constant promptings and make the right decision for her. Her free will has not been compromised. However, if she is praying for the same thing, then feel free to cross that line.

Is there power and strength in numbers? We know what happens at the time of tragedy when someone is killed unexpectedly. Faithful friends and families of the one affected all send out a common prayer of comfort. That comfort is definitely felt. My cousin and his wife lost their fifteen-year old daughter in a motor vehicle incident several years ago. They told me that they had unexplainable comfort at the time of the funeral and the days surrounding it, no doubt thanks to the prayers of others. However, as time went on, they could feel the prayers lessen as people went back to their normal lives. It made them realize that one prayer made a difference. They now have become a rock and a pillar for others who have suffered a similar loss. Others need our prayers long after we think they do.

In summary, the important thing to remember when we pray is to make sure that our level of faith matches our words spoken to God. He hears the words of our petition, but the level of faith or belief that He is, He can, and He will is what makes our prayer effective.

Prayer and meditation with faith takes us from surviving to thriving, from fear to love, from bondage to liberty, and from separation to connection.

Fellowship and Communion

God has planned that we spend time in fellowship with those who are like-minded and who aspire for higher faith so we can encourage and refresh each other.

First John 1:7 reads, "But if we walk in the light, as he is in the light, we have fellowship one with another, and the blood of Jesus Christ his Son cleanseth us from all sin."

Paul says in Acts 27:3, "And the next day we touched at Sidon. And Julius courteously entreated Paul, and gave him liberty to go unto his friends to refresh himself."

When our faith is at a low point and we are feeling discouraged in life, it is probably a good time to connect with high-faith friends. Paul, the apostle, often searched out his faithful friends for encouragement and refreshment. In Acts 21, we read of Paul sailing to Tyre, where he was met by some disciples who lavished care and encouragement on him for seven days. We then read of the families accompanying him to the edge of the city, where they prayed with him at the shore before sending him off on the ship.

Then in Acts 27, as a falsely accused prisoner held captive by the Romans, Paul was granted permission to visit his friends while en route to Rome from Jerusalem to await trial. Paul's faithful brethren encouraged him in his journey at a seemingly low time in his life, when he was facing strong persecution.

When we are facing adversity and feeling distressed, our ego might want to seek justification with other low vibrators. But at these times, positive influences are what we actually require. Choose your friends carefully. Do they contribute to your greater purpose or take away from it?

What if you are feeling stuck living in a negative environment that does not lend itself to spiritual connectedness? Let the energy shift begin with you. If your faith feels too low to connect with God, and no one else is around to encourage you, then minister to yourself to bring up your vibration first. Remember, we have to have *at least* a measure of faith to pray effectively to God to believe that He is, He can, and He will.

In 1 Samuel 30, David had no positive influences to turn to when his reality looked pretty grim. He and his men came home from battle feeling defeated and deflated only to find their hometown scorched with fire and raided, and their families taken by the Amalekites. As distressed as David already was at losing his family and his belongings, his own men then turned on him and were ready to stone

Application of the Law of Faith

him in their own grief. It is almost as if David's faith was weakened because he did not turn to God right away. He had ministered to and encouraged himself first.

In Psalms 42:11, David asks, "Why art thou cast down, O my soul? and why art thou disquieted within me? hope thou in God: for I shall yet praise him, who is the health of my countenance, and my God."

Everyone was against David and he felt defeated, but he remembered God and all he had to be thankful for. It seems that he could not even pray to God at this point because his faith was so weak. So I love that David ministered to himself to build up his faith. After this, he was able to pray to God, and then he and his men went on to win the battle against the Amalekites and bring their families back.

It is good to be aware of positive and negative influences in our life. We can appreciate communion or fellowship with others who are like-minded. They can encourage us and help restore our faith when we are at our weakest points.

Even when we find ourselves alone, we are not really alone if we have faith. Mary Magdalene thought she was all alone in her grief at the sepulcher after Jesus died on the cross (John 20). Little did she realize that Jesus was right there with her (she thought He was the gardener) along with two angels. We will never be or *feel* alone as long as we are in communion with our divine team and others of like mind.

Connect with the Earth

Have you ever wondered why so many people are drawn to oceans, lakes, mountains, or forests? Why do so many go camping as a vacation? Why are oceanfront properties and mountain retreats in such high demand? The thing that draws people to nature is more than the pretty scenery. We are drawn because nature consists of high-vibrating energy, which our inner being naturally gravitates toward.

When you strike a tuning fork, the air around it vibrates, sending out very strong vibrating impulses through the air. It does not take long before all other energies nearby rise until they resonate with the vibration of the fork. So it is with nature, which is like the tuning fork. When we come in contact with it, our vibration rises. We feel better; we relax and unwind. After a week or two at a lake, we feel better prepared to go back to the busyness of our lives.

The raw earth emits a magnetic energy as we connect with it, which recharges our inner batteries. How much time do you actually spend in a day touching God's creation and getting this much-needed energy boost? What if you change your gym treadmill workout to running through the park instead? What if you were to eat your lunch on

Application of the Law of Faith

the lawn during lunch hour instead of in the lunchroom or at a restaurant? Growing a vegetable or flower garden is a wonderful way to absorb this boost. We also absorb this energy when connecting with animals—horseback riding, playing with pets, etc. There have been positive results[2] for convicted prisoners when they connect with dogs during supervised training programs.

Job 12:7–10 reads as follows:

> But ask now the beasts, and they shall teach thee; and the fowls of the air, and they shall tell thee: Or speak to the earth, and it shall teach thee: and the fishes of the sea shall declare unto thee. Who knoweth not in all these that the hand of the LORD hath wrought this? In whose hand is the soul of every living thing, and the breath of all mankind.

What does connecting with the earth have to do with increasing our faith? It raises our vibration frequency. That is our goal. We do not worship nature, but we see God in it, and He receives the glory. We are closer to God's love when we are in nature because our vibration frequency increases. It is easier to be in the present moment when

---

[2] See www.karmarescue.org/paws-for-life.

we are surrounded by His handiwork. Try to use all your senses when you look around. Smell the odors, see the sights, touch the objects, and hear the sounds of nature. God loves it when we are in the moment of gratitude, thanking Him for the beautiful gift of creation for us to enjoy. Also, yoga can be very helpful in bringing us into the present moment to mindfulness and awareness.

Food and Health

What does food have to do with faith? Different foods have a unique vibration frequency, which affects our health and energy. We want to raise our vibration and eat foods that will contribute to that. As you might have guessed, the foods with the highest vibration frequency are high-alkaline vegetables and fruits such as beets, broccoli, kale, spinach, berries, melons, and lemons. Fermented foods and essentials oils are right up there in frequency as well.

In 1992, Bruce Tainio, plant geneticist, of Tainio Technology,[3] an independent division of Eastern State University in Cheney, Washington, developed the BT3 Frequency Monitoring System to measure the frequencies his plants were emitting.[4] The frequency monitor opened up many avenues of discovery in the area of frequencies

---

[3] See http://www.tainio.com/index.php?pageControl=about.
[4] See http://www.zoominfo.com/p/Bruce-Tainio/6467701.

and their effects first on plants, and later on animals and humans. The frequency monitor became a valuable tool in proving and explaining that every living thing has an energy field that is measurable. Each different frequency can affect those energy fields either positively or negatively, which in turn has significant effects on the health of the organism.

Tainio had determined that the average frequency of the human body during the daytime is 62–68 Hz. A healthy body frequency is 62–72 Hz. When the frequency drops, the immune system is compromised. The following are his findings:

<u>Human Body</u> (1 Megahertz [MHz] = 1 million cycles per second)

- Genius brain frequency: 80–90 MHz
- Brain frequency range: 72–90 MHz
- Normal human body: 62–78 MHz
  - From neck up: 72–78 MHz
  - From neck down: 62–68 MHz

Thyroid and parathyroid glands: 62–68 MHz
Thymus gland: 65–68 MHz
Heart: 67–70 MHz
Lungs: 58–65 MHz
Liver: 55–60 MHz

Pancreas: 60–80 MHz

Colds and flu start at: 57–60 MHz
Disease starts at: 58 MHz
Candida overgrowth starts at: 55 MHz
Receptive to cancer at: 42 MHz
Death begins at: 25 MHz[5]

Foods (1 Hertz [Hz] = 1 cycle per second)
(Fresh foods and herbs can be higher if grown organically and eaten freshly picked)

Fresh foods: 20–27 Hz
Fresh herbs: 20–27 Hz
Dried foods: 15–22 Hz
Dried herbs: 15–22 Hz
Processed/canned food (the majority of food eaten): 0 Hz

According to Dr. Royal R. Rife, a scientist and the inventor of the powerful Universal Microscope[6] in the late 1920s, every disease has a frequency. He found that certain frequencies can prevent the development of disease and that others can destroy disease. Substances with a higher

---

[5] See http://www.tainio.com and http://justalist.blogspot.ca/2008/03/vibrational-frequency-list.html.

[6] See http://web.archive.org/web/20100724091033/http://www.sangraal.com/rife.htm.

frequency will destroy diseases of a lower frequency. The study of frequencies raises an important question concerning the frequencies of substances we eat, breathe, and absorb.

After studying some of the various charts of food vibration frequencies, I found it most interesting that pork and aquatic bottom feeders such as shellfish (includes lobster, clams, crabs) are in the lowest vibrating category. It is a little more understandable to me now why God forbade the Israelites to eat these foods in Leviticus 11 of the Old Testament.

The Old Testament laws, which included dietary prohibitions, were done away with when Jesus came. Jesus wanted the focus to be more on what was going on in the heart instead of the stomach. In New Testament days, he gives his people complete freewill choice on what to eat and drink.

Mark 7:18–19 reads, "And he [Jesus] saith unto them, Are ye so without understanding also? Do ye not perceive, that whatsoever thing from without entereth into the man, it cannot defile him; Because it entereth not into his heart, but into the belly, and goeth out into the draught, purging all meats?"

Having said this, we know that our food affects our physical health and wellness. What affects us on one plane will eventually show up on the other two planes. By choosing healthy food, we are in a better frame of mind

Application of the Law of Faith

physically, mentally, and spiritually because we vibrate at a higher frequency. If you are feeling sad or depressed, you might want to choose high-vibrating fruits and vegetables instead of pork or shellfish.

Paul says in 1 Corinthians 10:23, "All things are lawful for me, but all things are not expedient: all things are lawful for me, but all things edify not."

Even though we have free will, it is wise to choose that which is in our best interest, such as healthy food and a healthy lifestyle.

Alcohol and almost all drugs vibrate at a low frequency. Along with the actual substances vibrating low, the atmosphere with which alcohol sometimes is associated is often low vibrating. The more we partake in low-vibrating activities of the ego, the further we are distancing ourselves from the love of God.

Be present with your food, and be mindful of each mouthful. Not only will you enjoy food more as you become aware of the unique flavors and textures, but also you will eat slower. Therefore, you will eat less food and consume fewer calories. [7] If the stomach actually takes twenty minutes to "figure out" that it is full, then what does that mean in terms of weight loss? Try to eat when you can take the time to be present with your food.

---

[7] See http://greatist.com/health/ask-expert-will-eating-slowly-help-me-lose-weight.

Sometimes, we might have to eat while we work or eat on the run while we are driving. This is part of life, but we must not make it a habit if we can help it. My sense is that overeating happens easily when people munch while watching a movie, watching a sporting event, or reading a book—and at other times when they are not present with their food.

When you are present with your food, then you are also present with your dining companions, so it is beneficial from multiple standpoints.

Power of Intention

Lynne McTaggert, a scientific investigative journalist, conducted an Intention Study in partnership with the University of Arizona, using seeds.[8] The goal was to see what would happen if a large group of people had the same thought at the same time. The scientists in Arizona prepared four sets of trays with freshly planted seeds. They took a photo of each labeled tray, which they sent on to Lynne, who was facilitating the Intention session in Australia at the time. Someone from her audience chose one of the four photos randomly, and the large audience sent the intention for growth of the seeds to that particular

---

[8] For more information, go to http://theintentionexperiment.com/wp-content/uploads/2011/01/germination-experiment.pdf.

tray in the photograph. Meanwhile, the scientists back in Arizona, who did not know which tray was selected, measured growth every five days on the four trays, which were all treated the same. This experiment was done in several other cities as well.

The results of the study are as follows: As an overall average, the seeds that were sent intention grew shoots 56 millimeters in height, compared with 48 millimeters for the untargeted seeds. This means that the seeds sent intention, on average, had shoots that were 8 millimeters (about a third of an inch, or 17 percent more) taller. In one case, the plants on the tray that was sent intention grew twice as high. It is interesting to note that intention was not sent from the same room to the physical tray of seeds, but from halfway around the world to a photograph of the physical object.

What does this mean for us in our everyday lives? When we understand the power of intention, we can let it spur us on to send intentions, in total and complete faith, into the unknown. After we set a firm intention, we wait for clarity to come as to which direction we should go. Again, follow what is light for you.

I like to send good intentions to each of my kids before they write a major university exam. In fact, some of them will remind me to send them good wishes just before they go in to write. Of course, they have to know the material, and things are brought to their remembrance at the right time. If they do not know the material, then it cannot be brought to their remembrance. I believe the good intentions just give them a little extra bit of positive energy. So it is.

When my oldest son was in his first year of law school, he told me about a pro bono program that he was hoping would accept him, where the student consulted directly with clients under the supervision of a practicing lawyer. He did not think his chances of being chosen for this program were high because of the high competition among first-year students. I thought I would have a bit of fun with setting an intention, so I sent the question off into the unknown: *I wonder what it would it take for him to get chosen for the pro bono program?* To his surprise, he was accepted into the program.

The secret recipe for actualizing an intention is to be happy and content with who you are in the present moment while maintaining a specific desire. When you feel so whole and complete that you no longer care whether *it* will happen, that is when amazing things will come together for you. It is as we set a clear intention and send it off into the unknown with complete trust in the outcome that the unexpected will begin to unfold as our intention becomes manifested. Avoid attaching "needy" emotion to your desire.

Sometimes we might set an intention and it does not appear to be manifesting. Why? We believe it will happen and it feels right and light, so why has it not happened yet? Our youngest son sent out an intention to land a job in a specific US city for a summer internship. He acted on inspirations that came, called some contacts, and applied for various positions. Doors just did not seem to open for him, even though he sent intention and felt light about it. He ended up taking a job in our home province with a smaller firm in his industry that summer. The knowledge and practical application he gained with this local company was incredible in spite of the downturn in the economy. As it turned out, it was the invaluable experience that he gained there that landed him a job in the US city of his choice a year later. Looking back now, he knows that he was not ready for the job that first summer. On the spiritual side, he knows he needed that summer to prove his faith to God. He went through some experiences in those months that took his faith to the next level, where he learned to have complete trust in the outcome. He knew what he had to do, and that summer was the time to do it. He let go of a lot of attachments that were holding him back. Now, he will be more than ready and strong enough to handle his new position. God knows exactly what we need and at just the right time. My son's intention did not change, but the

Application of the Law of Faith

timing of the outcome was a little different than expected, as there was a bit more he had to learn first.

Your inner guidance always knows best. What is best for us will show up as we ask in faith. Trust the process. Set an intention, believe it, and it will be so, according to your faith.

High-Vibration Music

We all know that music has the power to affect our emotions. Songs can make us cry or can make us feel like we are on top of the world.

Like everything else, sounds have a vibration frequency. Low-pitch tones have a low frequency, and high-pitched tones have a high frequency. Since we know that music has the power to influence our emotions, it stands to reason that we can use music as a tool to raise our vibration. When you are in a low-vibration state (depressed, angry, fearful, or anxious), you can simply pick higher-pitched-vibration songs that will help to elevate your spirits. Some examples of popular solo artists with high-vibration music are Jackie Evancho, Celine Dion, Enya, and Josh Groban.

Be mindful of the messages in your songs. Some songs have an uplifting message, and some songs do not. If you want to raise your vibration, it is best to pick songs that are about empowerment, love, and happiness over songs that focus on depression, anger, hate, or sadness.

Hymns carry high-vibrating messages. It might be good to keep in mind that the slower the hymns are sung, the lower their vibration, so you might not want to drag out the singing of these songs. If you listen close, you might even hear the angels join in. They love singing. If you believe it, you will hear them. If you do not believe, you will not hear them.

God loves singing. There are at least sixty-two verses in the Bible about singing. Colossians 3:16 reads, "Let the word of Christ dwell in you richly in all wisdom; teaching and admonishing one another in psalms and hymns and spiritual songs, singing with grace in your hearts to the Lord." James 5:13 reads, "Is any among you afflicted? let him pray. Is any merry? let him sing psalms."

As I referenced the Scriptures on singing, it was evident to me that singing gives birth to joy and joy gives birth to singing. Persistently in Scripture, joy and singing are bound together.

Elevate Your Thoughts, Behaviors, and Language

We all know now that positive thoughts are good for us and take us to a higher vibration, and that negative thoughts take us farther away from the love of God because of their

Application of the Law of Faith

low energy vibration. How do I elevate my thoughts when negative thoughts keep coming uninvited? How do I get victory over my thoughts?

First, we need to understand that years of the same type of thought and behavior patterns build grooved pathways in parts of our brain. Therefore, these same thoughts or behaviors become our default position and a matter of habit. Perhaps the first step to take when changing these patterns is to understand that they are habits. We must bring them from the subconscious into the conscious mind before we can change them.

What is a habit? A habit is formed when the body becomes the mind and the person is not making a choice with his or her conscious mind. Take time to notice what your habits are. Some of our habits are harmless, and some are not. Pause when you catch yourself doing something subconsciously. This will bring the habit from the subconscious to the conscious mind. An example might be opening the fridge door without consciously thinking about it. Pause and be aware as you notice your body taking over. Regain control of the moment and your body, and choose then if you actually want to open the fridge door or do something different. Be present and own each moment.

The more you practice with these tools, the sooner you will see results. Be patient with yourself, and understand that this process is two steps forward, one step back. Your backward steps might seem overwhelming, and you might feel like you have fallen off the progress train. This may be so, but remember that you are one stop farther up the track, and you will get back on again.

Speak and create new subconscious brain paths: You can begin retraining the subconscious with spoken positive language, which will begin to create new brain pathways. The more you speak these positive words, the deeper the new grooves will become as your beliefs change. This will take some time and practice, because the ego wants to reassume its default position and do what it has always done. Remember not to attach emotion to the old thoughts as they float by. The less emotion you attach, the less frequently the thoughts will come. A common principle in neuroscience says that neurons that fire together, wire together.[9] The more fire or emotion you give to the thoughts, the more wired and programmed you will become to have the same thoughts recur over and over. Therefore, if you repeatedly think and act in identical ways on a daily basis, then your brain will become molded into a specific hardwired pattern that will support the same level of mind. Many people hope that something different will

---

[9] For more about this, see http://www.drdomm.com/neurons-the-fire-together-wire-together/.

show up in their life, even though they think and do the same things day after day.

Do not own your ego's negative thoughts: Be only an observer to your thoughts. If the thought *I am so unhappy* comes into your mind, try to picture it floating by in a cloud caption and say, "That's an interesting thought." Try not to fight the thought, because you will only be putting negative emotional attachment to it, which will attract more of the same type of thoughts. When you learn to stand back and observe your thoughts from the third person, then your greater being (which is the real you) regains power over the thought. You can then make a conscious decision to change your thought, or speak over top of your thought, or go beyond your thought to the present moment, where inspiration and reason come. Once you attach emotion to the thought, the ego owns it and the same thought will recur over and over. The less attention and emotion you can give to the thought, the less amplitude it will have. If you can stand back and observe the thought in a neutral stance with detachment, then your greater being has the power. You then have power to choose an elevated thought as you remain neutral.

The apostle Paul says in Philippians 4:8, "Finally, brethren, whatsoever things are true, whatsoever things are honest, whatsoever things are just, whatsoever things are pure, whatsoever things are lovely, whatsoever things are of good report; if there be any virtue, and if there be any praise, think on these things."

Give gratitude: As previously mentioned, the more you give thanks to God for all things, the more quickly you will move into a positive place, which will affect your thoughts. Gratitude immediately elevates us. I cannot stress enough the importance of gratitude.

In Philippians 4:6–7, Paul says, "Be careful for nothing; but in every thing by prayer and supplication *with thanksgiving* let your requests be made known unto God."

Ask empowering questions: Elevate your thoughts and communication by asking powerful open-ended questions. The quality of your life mirrors the quality of your communication. When you elevate your communication, you elevate your reality. When you make statements or judgments, you limit your experience. When you ask questions, you are opening up awareness for other possibilities in your life.

When you find yourself making a judgment about yourself or another, *stop!* Switch that judgment to a question that would open up new possibilities. Example: Instead of making a judgment about how sad and unhappy you are in your marriage, turn that thought into an empowering question to God instead: "What would it take for a rich and meaningful experience to show up in my life that will bring my husband and me closer together?" Instead of grumbling about your boss, ask instead, "What can I do that would improve my relationship with my boss?" Do not look for answers. Clarity will come at the right time.

Stay in the question! Keep asking questions aloud to God—asking, asking, asking—throughout the day, and be alert for new opportunities, ideas, clarity, inspirations, etc., that show up. It may happen quickly, or it may take a while. *Do not look for answers* or try to guess how your opportunity will show up. When you come to a conclusion or find an "answer," you prevent new possibilities from showing up. The purpose of asking questions is to create possibilities and awareness, not answers! When we think we know best and make a firm decision without being open to all unknown possible options, then we limit ourselves. Perhaps God wants to show us something far better than we would even think to ask for. If we stay in the question, then what is best for us will show up.

If you are not happy with your job, you might ask, "What would it take for a new job or career to show up that would add to my learning and abundance?" Be prepared for anything, because it just might happen that you get fired first, which will then force you to open yourself up to new possibilities. Remember, something bad might happen first before something good shows up, so welcome each experience, good or bad, knowing that God is working behind the scenes for you.

I had a doubting Thomas come to me the other day and say, "Mom, I have been asking for weeks, 'What would it take?', and I still cannot get into the class I need." Sometimes when we are in the middle of an experience, it is very difficult not to attach ego emotion to our request. My son was frustrated and seemed to hit roadblocks everywhere he turned. I helped him out and sent a clear intention. Lo and behold, he called me that same afternoon and asked "Mom, how did you do it? I got into that class!" There were nine people ahead of him who needed that particular class to graduate, so he was originally told that he would not even be considered because he was a year behind them. It helped me to be specific in the request, because it was a prerequisite class he needed before he headed over to Hong Kong for the January semester. In certain situations like this, you might have to be specific in your request. However, if you are still stuck after being specific, then rethink your position and change up your request to something open-ended. Maybe something even better will emerge after that. Sometimes it is helpful to stand back and become an observer of the situation. That helps neutralize your position, as you give your power away when you become attached to specific outcomes, situations, or things.

Similarly, our eldest son was struggling with his course schedule for one class in his law program. I suggested to him to put logic and emotion aside, to use intention, and

Application of the Law of Faith

then wait and see what shows up. I followed up a few days later to discover that clarity had come to him about a self-led class option of his choice. When we send intention that is free of emotional attachment, what is best for us will show up. So it is, according to our faith.

Our daughter was looking for day care for her two little ones when she headed back to college. The specific home that she was asking for was not opening up for her. I suggested that she be open to other possibilities, and rephrase the question so that it would be more open-ended and might attract something even better. So she asked, "What would it take for a day care home to show up that operates with my own values and would be a loving and wholesome natural environment for the children?" Within days, a new home opened up to her that more than met her expectations. Wow, how does it get any better than that? Her ultimate need was fulfilled in an unexpected way because she was open-minded.

Here is an example of asking a powerful question, trusting, and then not being concerned about *how* the answer will show up. My husband and I received an unexpected government tax bill that we hadn't allowed for in our budget. I sent out the question, "What would it take for $35,000 to actualize within the next few weeks?" I then left the matter with God, totally trusting that it would be taken care of. I did not think about it again until two weeks later. My husband and I were driving home from a conference in Manitoba when the neighbor to our Alberta ranch called to say that our shop had burned down. We soon received a check from our insurance agency for $37,290. I would never have expected the money to show up that way. It is not up to us to figure out the how or the why. My husband was out a shop, but it all worked out in the end. We do not know the big picture, nor do we need to. We had leased out the shop to people who, we now know, were questionable tenants. Who knows what could have happened in the future? Perhaps this solution saved us from a lot of future grief. We can be glad that a far greater intelligence does see the big picture, and that all we have to do is trust that all is well.

Did God care about the $35,000? Perhaps not, but I believe that He picked up on my faith that the situation would be resolved, and then my faith or energy attracted a solution. If we do not ask a question in faith, then we will not receive in faith. Jesus told us many times to ask with faith. After we ask, we must be aware of new inspirations or of doors opening, and then we should move forward, following what feels light and right.

Ego thoughts are a perception. What are *true* thoughts? True thoughts are inspired by our inner-guidance team. If a thought is not true, then what is it? It must be

Application of the Law of Faith

an illusion or a perception of the ego. We will return to this idea.

"What is truth?" Pilate asked Jesus this question. Perhaps Christians would say the short answer is, "Jesus is Truth, because he is the Way, the Truth, and the Life!" He is the human expression of God, who is the Source of all truth. Perhaps another way to describe it is that truth is the reality—spiritual and universal—that God created and defined. The Holy Spirit within us guides us toward all truth. Jesus's words are true because they are in accordance to the truth and reality of God.

If we asked Pilate, "What is truth?", he might have answered, "Truth is Rome, soldiers, armies, Caesar, political power." He perceived those things to be his truth, but they were not his absolute truth. The only absolute truth in Pilate's life was the part of him that was lined up with, or that conformed to, the truth and reality of God, which would come through his inner guidance system. We read of one true thought Pilate had when he said, "I find no fault in this man," referring to Jesus, in Luke 23:4. This thought would have come from his inner guidance. However, he chose to listen to his ego and to silence the voice of his conscience. The parts of our lives that are true are those that line up with the truth and reality of God. They will reveal themselves through our conscience, intuition, and gut feeling.

Some folks say that science is truth. Science is true when it acknowledges what God Himself has already defined and established from the beginning. True thoughts are lined up to God's reality and truth. Every other thought is our own perception. We might think our thought is true, because it seems very real to us. Our perceived thoughts are formed from past experiences which determine our perception of reality.

Let us observe our thoughts again. What percentage of your current thoughts are from past experiences, such as people you talked to yesterday, the argument you just had with your teenager, the conversation you had with your cousin, a hectic day at work, etc.? What percentage of your thoughts are about the future—events you are planning, work deadlines, etc.? What percentage of your thoughts are in the present moment? Note: true thoughts come *only* when we are present.

If our thoughts are centered on our fear of world events and horrors, then that is what we will see in the news. Our thoughts come first, and then we see what we believe. If we are suspicious, then we assume that other people are untrusting, too. None of those thoughts are true and accurate, because God only puts true thoughts of love, peace, truth, and joy in us. Therefore, thoughts of fear, doubt, and suspicion must be a mere perception of the ego.

Proverbs 3:5 reads, "Trust in the Lord with all thine heart; and lean not unto thine own understanding."

We all have our perceived thoughts because we all have ego. The first step in overcoming them is to observe them and recognize them for what they are, namely, perception and illusion based on past experiences. If we recognize this, then we can look beyond these thoughts to the peace and truth just beyond.

Exercise: This might be a helpful prayer. "Dear Father, I understand that my own perceptions are not in my own best interests! Thank You for helping me to see through Your eyes so that my thoughts can be true."

Chapter 3

WHAT HINDERS THE LAW OF FAITH

I now understand how to increase my faith and my vibration frequency to attract experiences into my life that will contribute joyfully to my life purpose. What are some of the biggest challenges that might hinder me from ascending to a higher faith or consciousness?

Judgment

We must stay out of judgment. In chapter 1 and 2, we are reminded to stay in the question mode, because it opens up new possibilities. Similarly, when we judge ourselves or others, we shut down possibilities because we have already made a conclusion or statement. We cannot receive beyond what we have concluded.

Here is an example of what I mean. If you make a negative statement to your spouse and say, "You are so selfish and uncaring of how I feel," then you are empowering that idea and might actually solidify it. You would not be contributing to new possibilities for your spouse to be inspired to change. You might say instead, "I love it when you consider me before making decisions because it shows me how much you care"—or something similar.

Speak to your spouse or significant other as though he is already what you desire. You may soon notice a change in him, but it is most likely that *your* vision has changed. One young wife was telling me that she noticed that her husband became much more caring and attentive once she became more aware of the power of her language. I had to smile. Her husband very well could have been responding to her positive language, but my guess is that her language very much affected *her* own vision of what she saw in him.

Talk to your children as though they are already what you desire or expect. Trust them first and they will be trustworthy. Give them responsibility and they will be responsible. I knew someone who would often accuse her children of lying, and so they did because it was expected of them. My husband and I tried to speak to our kids as if they were honest, and so they were for the most part. It was an infrequent occurrence that they did not tell the truth, so when they lied, their faces could not hide it.

My father taught me a great lesson on trusting one's kids. Handing me his credit card as I left for Australia as an eighteen-year-old, he said, "Use this if you need to." This showed me how much he trusted me, so I made sure I did not abuse his trust. Later, when I left home to move to another city, he gave me a blank check and said, "Use this if you need it." I remember making the mistake of telling my roommate that I had this check. Within a few days of moving in, she had gone to different garage sales, where she had bought furniture and put it on hold. I asked her how we were going to pay for it, as I had barely started my new job. She reminded me of my dad's check. I then took the check and ripped it up. My purpose in telling this story is not to earn accolades but, rather, to emphasize that trust breeds trustworthiness.

When we judge our children negatively, we are actually stunting their personal growth and limiting their opportunities. Hand over your car keys to your teenage son and tell him that you trust him. Try to avoid telling him all the things that could potentially go wrong, lest you solidify those. Trust him first. If he abuses your trust, then use more caution the next time. Our words are powerful. Let us choose them wisely.

Given my awareness, I cringe when I hear someone say, "Wow, it doesn't get any better than this!" Even though the person likely means this in a positive way, I find it to be a very limiting statement. Turn this judgment into an empowering question: "Wow, how does it get any better than this?" When you send this question off into the unknown, you might be surprised at what shows up to make things even better.

As I sat through a funeral of a teenage girl who committed suicide, I found myself judging the pastor who was officiating as being self-serving and attention-seeking. By judging and coming to a conclusion about him, I basically closed the door for being of any potential help to him should the opportunity arise. Jesus would have looked on this man in compassion, would have been open to help, and would not have shut down possibilities by judging the pastor negatively. As we learned from the widow woman in 2 Kings 4, God cannot give to us or use us beyond what our faith, judgments, and conclusions will allow.

Jesus said in Matthew 7:1–2, "Judge not, that ye be not judged. For with what judgment ye judge, ye shall be judged: and with what measure ye mete, it shall be measured to you again."

Jesus asked us not to judge because it limits our faith in what can be done in us and through us. We cannot become or be used beyond our own rule of measure.

There are many unconscious judgments we have about ourselves that we are not even aware of, like believing we are unattractive, believing we are undeserving, or having feelings of unworthiness. By having those thoughts and feelings, we are empowering them by attracting more of the same low-vibration thoughts and feelings.

Some of us confuse feelings of unworthiness with humility. The main difference between the two is where our focus is. When we feel unworthy, our focus is on us and how weak we feel. With humility, the focus is on God, Jesus, or others. We want humility in our life. The word *unworthy* is mentioned twice in the Bible, and both times it has a negative connotation. God wants us to rejoice in the fact that Jesus is worthy, to sing praises to Him, and to have joy and light in our lives because of it. Humility does not mean "thinking less of me" but rather "thinking about me less." John the Baptist was very close to missing out on one of the greatest privileges of humankind—baptizing Jesus—because his focus was on his own feelings of unworthiness rather than on the worthiness of Christ. Jesus lovingly reminded him that it was not about him (John), but that there was a bigger picture.

Matthew 3:13–15 reads, "Then cometh Jesus from Galilee to Jordan unto John, to be baptized of him. But John forbad him, saying, I have need to be baptized of thee, and comest thou to me? And Jesus answering said unto him, Suffer it to be so now: for thus it becometh us to fulfill all righteousness. Then he suffered him."

It is good to be aware of our own judgments, even self-judgments. It helps to use questions to open up possibilities for us and to free up others for new possibilities as well.

We want to stay out of judgment, but we do want to have discernment. Discernment is taking instruction from a *situation* for our own soul, and learning, but it does not include judging the *person*. I love the *Oxford Dictionaries* definition of *discernment*: "perception in the absence of judgment with a view to obtaining spiritual direction and understanding."[1]

In Proverbs 24:30–32, we read about the man who walked by the field of the slothful. He took instruction for himself and went on his way. He did not seek out the owner of the field and reprimand him or judge him. The verses read as follows: "I went by the field of the slothful, and by the vineyard of the man void of understanding; And, lo, it was all grown over with thorns, and nettles had covered the face thereof, and the stone wall thereof was broken down. Then I saw, and considered it well: I looked upon it, and received instruction."

When we judge ourselves or others, it actually becomes a faith issue, because it limits the possibilities of what God can do in our lives. If we have made conclusions, then God cannot give us anything beyond our own rule of measure.

---

[1] OxfordDictionaries.com, s.v. "discernment," http://www.oxforddictionaries.com/definition/american_english/discernment.

Unrepentant Sin

What is sin? Sin is anything that takes us away from the high vibration of God's love. Provision has been made for believers, according to our faith.

Does God see our sin, or does He look at the believers through the blood of Christ?

Paul says in 2 Corinthians 5:21, "For he hath made him to be sin for us, who knew no sin; that we might be made the righteousness of God in him."

Whether or not God sees the sins of His believers, He knows when we have sinned, because we have moved away from His love. When we indulge in low-vibration activities and thoughts, we separate ourselves from the high vibration of His love. God has not gone anywhere. He has not left us, but rather we have chosen to move downward to a lower consciousness, bringing separation.

How do we repent? Repentance is acknowledging our state or where we are, and then turning toward His love. It is more than saying, "I am sorry." It is an action of turning and believing. God loves a repentant soul who turns toward His love with the guidance of the Holy Spirit. The Holy Spirit is constantly redirecting the believers back on course to a higher consciousness.

What is an example of sin? Not forgiving someone is an example of a sin because we would have heavy low vibration emotions such as hate. Sin is a low-vibration thought, act, or feeling that hinders us from moving up into a higher consciousness. How do you repent from this sin? Forgive, turn, and believe, and then move on with your life. What if it is not that easy? Begin with giving gratitude to God for all things. Then ask an empowering question: "What would it take for the relationship to heal?" or something similar. You will gradually feel yourself healing from your hurt and anger. The higher your faith, the more love you will feel. Hate or anger cannot exist in a heart filled with gratitude and love. Put your time and focus on increasing your faith with gratitude and acceptance. Lack of forgiveness and other sins take away from our abundance on all levels.

Is there a hell for unrepentant sinners? The Bible definitely talks about a reality of torment; however, it was never meant for the souls of humankind. Rather, it was prepared for the devil and his angels. As Jesus said in Matthew 25:41, "Then shall he [God] say also unto them on the left hand, Depart from me, ye cursed, into everlasting fire, **prepared for the devil and his angels**".

Even though humankind has free will, it was always God's intention that *all* souls would come to repentance, acknowledge Him and His Son, and turn from their wicked ways. Faith is very much part of this acknowledgement.

It reads in 2 Peter 3:9, "The Lord is not slack concerning his promise, as some men count slackness; but is longsuffering to us-ward, *not willing that any should perish, but that all should come to repentance*".

God has made every provision for humankind to come to know Him now through faith, so that we will know eternity with Him in a heavenly realm. It is not He who sends the faithless and the wicked to torment, but it is our freewill choice to believe or not to believe that determines our soul's destiny. Can we expect to spend eternity with God in love if we do not believe that He is, He can, or He will? Revelation 21:8 reminds us that the faithless, fearful, and wicked will not escape the second death.

God gave us this world as a testing ground to experiment with faith and to learn to trust Him with the little things of everyday life so that we can come to trust Him with our soul and eventually partake of the fruit of the Spirit.

Fear, apathy, depression: We do not think of fear as being a sin, but it is the opposite of love on the faith scale. It is at the same vibration category as hate, shame, and guilt.

First John 4:18 reads, There is no fear in love; but perfect love casteth out fear: because fear hath torment. He that feareth is not made perfect in love."

We usually have fears because our inner being feels a separation from God's love, whether we understand it or not. It is not possible to be *perfectly* enveloped in the love of God and yet have consuming fears on the physical and mental planes. If we are trusting, then we cannot be fearing.

Isaiah 12:2 reads, "Behold, God is my salvation; I will trust, and not be afraid: for the Lord Jehovah is my strength and my song; he also is become my salvation."

Apathy or complacency is similar in vibration to fear. Being indifferent, not caring one way or the other, not placing importance on things that ought to be important, is also cause for alarm. In fact, Christian apathy is one of the most understated sinful conditions that goes unnoticed and unchecked, until we find that we have checked out completely. Has your *life* or Christian *service* to God become mechanical? This seemed to be the case for the Ephesian church in Revelation 2:4. They lost their first love. Their service was no longer motivated by love and had become a mere obligation. How do we turn from apathy? We turn the same way as we would from any other low-vibrating thought, feeling, or action. We build up our faith again, beginning with giving gratitude to God for all things. Turning to Him in gratitude is the first step to overcoming all forms of apathy, whether it is having no regard or care for the life and well-being of our fellow man, or not caring about our own soul. Gratitude immediately increases our level of faith and caring, one degree at a time.

Depression vibrates a bit lower than fear, but is in the same low dense-vibration category. The vibration of extreme depression is only a few degrees higher than the vibration of death. In cases of extreme depression, medical attention is necessary. Building your faith and using these universal tools takes time and commitment; it is not something that happens overnight. Medical help may be necessary to bring a patient back up to his or her base level before he or she can learn to tap into this universal flow.

The good news is that even though these low-level emotions and feelings are opposite from love and peace on the faith scale, we now know how to raise our vibration to a higher degree. Begin with gratitude and praise. Talk to God throughout your day, thank Him for what you are asking for, spend time with high-faith friends, speak your world into being by asking empowering questions, and connect with nature, music, etc. The more you practice and believe, the more goodness will show up in your life.

We need to be conscious of what is low-vibration sin. What adds to our faith and what takes away from it? Perhaps a good question to ask ourselves before we make a decision about where to go or what to do is, "Will this contribute to my faith or take away from it?" If you follow your inner guidance and are in tune with your lightness/heaviness, you will be led away from low-vibration sin and move toward your greater purpose.

The Bible tells us to fear God. Is this fear also low vibration? I want to clarify that ego-based emotional fear is very different from a healthy fear of God on the higher plane. To fear God simply means having high reverence and respect for Him. Psalms 111:10 reads, "The fear of the Lord is the beginning of wisdom: a good understanding have all they that do his commandments: his praise endureth for ever."

Claiming Other, Low Energies As Our Own

What if I am doing all the right things mentioned to increase my faith, including keeping away from low-vibration activities, yet I am still feeling vulnerable and fearful?

It seems to be that the most tenderhearted among us struggle the most with low-vibration thoughts and emotions, which lead to anxiety and depression. Why? One reason is that softhearted folks are sensitive and tend to take on low negative energies that do not belong to them. We may pick up these low energies from an angry driver in traffic, from screaming and fighting kids, from our grumpy, demanding supervisor, or from a depressed friend. The first step in changing this is to understand what is going on. Ask your greater being verbally, "Is this heaviness I feel really mine?" If it lightens up, then it is not yours. Either way, just ask the negative energy *to leave and not return* with intention. Remember how powerful your intentions can be if accompanied with belief. Repeat as necessary. Many people feel justified by their anger (low negative energy), thinking, for example, *She made me angry*. But know that we all have the power to choose our reactions and intentions. Jesus gave us an example of how to ask these low energies to leave with intention and belief.

Mark 9:25 reads, "When Jesus saw that the people came running together, he rebuked the foul spirit, saying unto him, Thou dumb and deaf spirit, *I charge thee, come out of him, and enter no more into him*".

Jesus makes it sound really simple. You will come to understand that life becomes simple when you add faith to your everyday living. In fact, when you finally figure out the power of belief, you might laugh at the simplicity of it all. Please understand that building up your faith does not happen overnight. You might have years' worth of negative buildup that you have to undo. Patience and constant practice is very important. Start asking (or thanking God) for something small that you can easily believe will come into fruition, have an "aha" moment, and then work up from there. At first, you might be pleasantly surprised at what shows up as a result of your request. As your faith increases, you might find you will be more surprised if something does *not* show up. Always give gratitude and praise to God for granting your request. This will stimulate the positive cycle even more.

These low-vibration energies get their strength by the faith we have in them to do us harm. This was the case with our son. He was taking on other people's negative energies and unknowingly claiming them as his own. Because of his kind and tender heart, he would pick up these energies from all around him: at school, from friends with problems. He would unknowingly soak it all up. His friends always felt better when they were around him. He had a few friends call him regularly with their troubles. They would leave uplifted, whereas he would feel burdened for days, not understanding why. It spiraled downhill from there. He believed he was doomed—and so he was, until his beliefs changed. Even as he began to understand how the process of coming to vibrate at a higher level worked, he still had to endure a year of trial and error before he finally learned how to keep the low energies at bay while still remaining open to his friends with a listening ear. He learned that empathy or sympathy were things he could not give. Compassion was the higher ground that he needed to take. Compassion only comes with a higher faith. That is what he had to work on.

Having empathy is to lower your vibration to the level of the one pouring out. This makes it so that you are better able to relate to the person's pain and suffering. Having compassion is to keep your higher level of vibration but to still have the care and love. Jesus always showed compassion and never lowered his level of faith or vibration to match the one pouring out. He never allowed anyone or anything to affect his faith, no matter what the situation was.

Matthew 9:36 reads, "But when he [Jesus] saw the multitudes, he was moved with compassion on them, because they fainted, and were scattered abroad, as sheep having no shepherd."

Ministers, pastors, priests, and community-service people who are regularly called upon to counsel individuals with problems, have to be careful about maintaining a vibration level higher than the one pouring out. They care very much about people, yet some may be unclear about how to keep low energies from taking hold of them. These low energies manifest themselves in the form of negative thoughts, depression, lack of energy, sadness, etc.

Half the battle is won if we understand how energy works. When you know you will be going into a potentially negative situation with family or friends, ask God (or thank Him) for His shield of protection around you. Visualize an invisible shield or a capsule around your whole body as you ask. It will be given to you according to your faith.

Dishonesty

Dishonesty is low-vibration energy regardless of how big or little the crime is. Whether you are being dishonest in a business transaction, are stealing from a store, or are lying to a friend for a selfish motive, it is all dishonesty. It is all the same to God.

Luke 16:10 reads, "He that is faithful in that which is least is faithful also in much: and he that is unjust in the least is unjust also in much."

Have you ever noticed that the people who are distrustful of others are often the ones who are the most distrustful themselves? Life is a mirror. We see in others what we are. Our outer world is a reflection of our inner world. The dishonest energy that we send out will be attracted back to us and manifested negatively. The money we try to save by being dishonest will catch up to us some way or another. We just might be surprised with unexpected bills and repairs somewhere else. Dishonesty breaks up our flow.

Paul says in 1 Timothy 2:2, "That we may lead a quiet and peaceable life in all godliness and honesty."

One might ask if it is honest when you thank God for what you are asking for, as if you have already received it. Your physical world is based on your perception of (believed) reality, so you have the power to believe what you will, according to your faith and soul guidance. Remember, your only *absolute* truth comes from your soul guidance. Everything else is your ego perception of what is true. Based on a medical doctor's truth, he might tell a patient that she has eighteen months to live. Sure enough, the patient believes the doctor, resigns herself to the prognosis, and dies within that time period. An alternative practitioner's truth might be that most of his patients heal when they are told they can heal. Our belief system is the placebo. Some people might even call this arrogance—to think that we can choose what to believe and it will come into fruition. Arrogance is of the ego. High faith equals low ego. It is this higher power, and our faith in it, that deserves the glory and praise for what we experience here and now in this life. Arrogance is about our ego self receiving the glory for our successes in life.

Honesty is being free from deceit and living with sincerity. Self-respect and honor comes with living an honest and peaceable life. Being honest is being true to our inner guidance system, which results in flow. Therefore, dishonesty not only hinders our faith but also stops our flow.

Chapter 4

LAW OF LOVE

The love and peace of God is the ultimate in high-frequency energy vibration that we can attain in this life. God's law of love is the law of miracles. Miracles cannot occur without the high-vibration atmosphere that accompanies an abundance of unconditional love. Unconditional love gives of itself without any thought of self.

In the Old Testament, God gave Moses the Ten Commandments for the Israelites to live by, along with a listing of ordinances. These are the commandments, in short form:

1. Thou shalt have no other gods before Me.
2. Thou shalt not make unto thee any graven images.
3. Thou shalt not take the name of the Lord your God in vain.
4. Remember the Sabbath day, to keep it holy.
5. Honor your father and your mother.

6. Thou shalt not murder.
7. Thou shalt not commit adultery.
8. Thou shalt not steal.
9. Thou shalt not bear false witness against your neighbor.
10. Thou shalt not covet.

You will notice that love is not mentioned at all. These commandments tested the obedience of the Israelites, but they did not test their love for God. It was not until Jesus came in the New Testament that the law of love was established.

Matthew 22:36–40 reads, "Master, which is the great commandment in the law? Jesus said unto him, *Thou shalt love the Lord thy God with all thy heart, and with all thy soul, and with all thy mind.* This is the first and great commandment. And the second is like unto it, *Thou shalt love thy neighbor as thyself.* On these two commandments hang all the law and the prophets".

The Ten Commandments were no longer required, because the law of love covered all of the commandments. If a Christian were truly dwelling in the love of God, then he would not kill, steal, commit adultery, or worship idols.

God Love

What does it mean to love God with our heart, soul, and mind? I believe it is an all-encompassing love that covers all parts of our lives—the physical, mental, and spiritual—like yeast in dough. We have ascended in consciousness and faith to reach the ultimate love of God. We have moved beyond human love and self-love. If we truly have this love of God, then it will be first place in our lives. All lower loves will fall into their natural healthy places.

As we come fully into God's high-vibration love, then our walk, words, and actions will naturally be in accordance with that love. So often we think we have to serve better or deny ourselves more before God can love and accept us. Rather than trying to serve better, perhaps we ought to love more. By default, everything will fall into place if we focus on love and on increasing our vibration. If we are operating within this high-vibrating love, then we will be naturally denying the ego by default. It is far better that our works are motivated by love than by duty and obligation.

The following verse is relevant to the love of God, even though the word itself is not mentioned in the verse. Jesus said in Matthew 6:22, "The light of the body is the eye: if therefore thine eye be single, thy whole body shall be full of light."

I have read this verse many times over the years, but I did not really understand it until recently. I believe Jesus is talking about having single vision vs. double vision.

What is double vision? Perhaps double vision is looking through the eyes of the ego and seeing duality around us. We could look at a person and see the good in her as well as the bad. We see the right and the wrong in the world. We see love and hate around us. As a result of Adam and Eve's sin in the Garden of Eden by partaking of the tree of the knowledge of good and evil, we see good and evil with this double vision.

What is single vision, then? I believe single vision is looking at the world and others through the spiritual eye of love (oneness). When we look at others, we no longer see duality, but we see the good in them. We see God in everything, even in our experiences of sorrow. There is a hymn with the words, "Precious thought ... joy and sorrow interwoven, love in all I see." The writer of this hymn truly had single vision. Single vision brings clarity, perspective, light, and joy. Compassion replaces negative judgment of others. Love replaces fear. Single vision is having an understanding that our ego thoughts are just clouds that float by, which we can observe but do not own. True single vision is looking beyond those thoughts and tapping into the mind of Christ, which is love, compassion, giving, receiving, forgiving, patience, humility, wisdom, virtuousness, etc. To have single vision is to be truly immersed in the love of God.

You will know your vision is changing when you start noticing a higher level of love and goodness in others around you. Perhaps asking God (or thanking Him) for new vision could be your most important prayer of the day!

Self-Love (Honor)

What did Jesus mean when He said to love your neighbor as yourself? What if you hate yourself? What would that mean for your neighbor? Before we can love our neighbor or others, we need to love and honor ourselves first. I do not think Jesus meant that you should love the human ego. I think He meant that you should love who you really are within, and love the miraculous body that you were given to house your soul.

The amount of love and appreciation you feel from God, your spouse, or others is directly proportionate to how much you are willing to honor and love yourself. You can only feel and therefore receive the amount of love from God and others that you feel you are worthy of. The rest is left on the table. This does not mean that the love is not being offered to you. It just means that you are unable to receive it, because you cannot receive more than your faith or belief system will allow. The quality of your relationship with yourself is reflected in every other relationship you have, and can even influence your level of confidence in trusting and respecting your inner guidance. Your Creator loves and appreciates you, more than you will ever know. His choice is to love you, whether you love or hate yourself. He rejoices when you love yourself, because loving you means loving Him, the One who created you. Again, if God is your first love, then love on these lower planes will naturally fall into its rightful place.

The honor and respect you have for yourself has a great influence over your thoughts. One reason we have negative thoughts is because we see ourselves in a negative light. This also leads to a negative outlook on the people and the world around us. Our outer world is a reflection of our inner world.

Following are two little exercises to help you improve your degree of self-love.

Exercise #1: Let's reprogram the subconscious! This might seem a bit weird at first, but it works! Remember, the subconscious does not know the difference between true and false. It believes that which it hears the most about.

In the morning and at night, stand in front of the mirror and say the following:

- I love you, [your name].
- I respect and honor you, [your name].
- I am very thankful for you, [your name].

How did it feel? If it was tough to look at yourself in the eyes while saying these words, then you could use a little more self-honor and self-respect.

Continue to practice this often until you can feel comfortable speaking these words to yourself. The purpose of this exercise is not to "puff up" your ego but to honor and respect God's handiwork in the beautiful vessel that you are. When you look at yourself through the eyes of your human ego, you will see duality, your imperfections and perfections (good and bad). If you look at yourself through the divine eye of love, you will see the miraculous vessel that you are. Honoring and respecting yourself is honoring and respecting God, the One who created you. In time, you will be built up in a healthy way, and you will be able to face any situation head-on, with confidence and resiliency. Over time, you will discover that loving and honoring yourself improves everything in your life, from your relationships, your health, and your well-being to your ability to manifest your dreams and your connection with God.

Exercise #2: This is known as the elastic band trick. Put an elastic band on your wrist in the morning. When you engage in negative self-talk or thoughts that do not honor you, your spouse, or others, snap the elastic. The purpose of this is that *you become aware that you are aware* of negative thoughts so that you can consciously change them to thoughts of gratitude, respect, and love. By becoming aware of being aware, you become an observer of your thoughts. We can only learn control when we do not take ownership of our ego's negative thoughts by attaching emotion to them.

Have fun with this! Keep it light!

Love for Others

Jesus says in John 13:34–35, "A new commandment I give unto you, That ye love one another; as I have loved you, that ye also love one another. By this shall all men know that ye are my disciples, if ye have love one to another."

The love we have for others is a measure of how well we are doing on the faith vibration scale. If we have any hardness or lack of forgiveness toward someone, then we know we are not even close to the love of God, where love is unconditional.

Jesus was our perfect example of loving others unconditionally. Why did Jesus call Judas a friend when He knew he was going to betray Him within hours? Why did He tell His Father to "forgive them because they know not what they do," referring to those who put him on the cross? Why? It was because He was completely filled with the love of God, which overruled all lower emotions and feelings in lower planes.

Law of Love

If there are no mandatory laws and ordinances anymore, then how do we treat others with love? What does this really mean in our everyday life?

Jesus says the following in Matthew 25:35–40:

> For I was an hungred, and ye gave me meat: I was thirsty, and ye gave me drink: I was a stranger, and ye took me in: Naked, and ye clothed me: I was sick, and ye visited me: I was in prison, and ye came unto me. Then shall the righteous answer him, saying, Lord, when saw we thee an hungred, and fed thee? or thirsty, and gave thee drink? When saw we thee a stranger, and took thee in? or naked, and clothed thee? Or when saw we thee sick, or in prison, and came unto thee? And the King shall answer and say unto them, Verily I say unto you, Inasmuch as ye have done it unto one of the least of these my brethren, ye have done it unto me.

These words do not express rules or commandments. Instead, they serve as a measuring stick, perhaps of where our love for others is. The more love of God we have within, the more we will reach out to others.

Chapter 5

LAW OF CIRCULATION (FLOW)

The law of circulation states that nothing is static; all things in the universe are always flowing in circulation. Energy flows in and out of everything. Flow is everywhere around us: in rivers, oceans, electrical currents, air, faucets, rain, lava, blood, tree sap, radio waves, and so on.

We are all stewards of the universe's resources. If you do not circulate what you have so it can further the work of the universe, then what you have will be taken away from you and then given to another who is doing so.

Positive circulation is when things increase in a positive way. Negative circulation is when things diminish. What you hold onto will keep slipping away until there is nothing left. You can never escape the law of circulation. If you try to stop the circulation of things, the circulation will still occur—but in a negative manner. It will be circulated through unexpected expenses such as paying for repairs and

Law of Circulation (Flow)

replacements of things that are damaged, stolen, or lost. Look at areas in your life where you feel stuck. What are you not letting go of?

Most people believe that they have to *get* before they can *give*, but we all have something we can give. We have time, energy, love, support, money, and more. Go visit your dear old aunt in the care home. Throw in a dime or quarter in the Starbucks tip jar, or add the extra dollar onto your grocery bill for the Children's Wish Foundation. Buy a coffee for the beggar on the street corner if you are not comfortable with giving him cash. Support the church or whatever charity you feel passionate about. You will come to understand that whatever you give, you will receive back tenfold, yet not always in kind. Since everything in the universe is continually circulating, what you give to someone is what you will get back—but in a different form and from a different source.

If you hoard things in life like money, material goods, ideas, or resentments, then flow stops, as there is no space for that which is new and positive to enter. To allow the new into your life, you must let go of the old.

Where there is flow, there is life. The Jordan River flows into the Sea of Galilee and then down to the Dead Sea. Marine life is plentiful in the Sea of Galilee. Splashes of green adorn its banks. Along its shores, children play, farms thrive, men build houses close by, and birds build nests in the surrounding vegetation.

The Jordan continues its flow down south into the Dead Sea. In this sea there is no splash of fish. There is no fluttering leaf, no song of birds, and no children's laughter on its banks. The air hangs heavy above its waters, and neither human nor beast nor fowl will drink from it.

If both seas are being fed the same healthy life source from the Jordan River, what makes the difference in these neighboring seas? Why does one give life and the other give death? Here is the difference. The Sea of Galilee receives, but does not keep, the water from the Jordan. For every drop that flows into it, another drop flows out. The giving and receiving go on in equal measure. In contrast, the Dead Sea greedily keeps every drop that flows into it from the Jordan and gives nothing away. It is flow that sustains life.

The Bible gives us very clear direction on how to keep flow moving, as discussed below.

Flow of Giving and Receiving

Jesus said in Luke 6:38, "Give, and it shall be given unto you; good measure, pressed down, and shaken together, and running over, shall men give into your bosom. For

Law of Circulation (Flow)

with the same measure that ye mete withal it shall be measured to you again."

Everything in life is flow. God loves flow. Open your heart and receive the abundance of love, grace, and goodness that He sends to you. You cannot pass it onto others unless you first receive it. When you truly receive it, let it flow through you to others. Remember the law about judgment. The moment you place judgment on another, the flow stops immediately with you. If we get stuck on judgments of ourselves, then this will also stop the flow. God does not like *blockages*. If we are truly open to giving and receiving, it is almost as if God looks down and says, "Here is a vessel I can use to accomplish My purpose for another." The more He gives and we pass on, the more we will receive. This law applies to everything on all three planes, from physical things to matters of the heart and soul.

Giving is often easier than receiving for some people. Receiving even a compliment for many is difficult. Not receiving interrupts the flow, however. It is like putting up a dam in a free-flowing river. If you do not receive, then you deny the other person the joy of giving. In relationships, allowing yourself to receive is crucial if you want a fulfilling and satisfying experience. Accept a gift from another with thanks. It is your turn to receive. When you refuse a gift from anyone, you are blocking not only

Law of Circulation (Flow)

the flow of abundance in your life but also the flow of abundance in the giver's life.

In Luke 6:34, Jesus said, "And if you lend to those from whom you expect repayment, what credit is that to you?" (NIV)

Give, expecting nothing in return from what you pass on to others! Just let what you have been given flow out onto others, whether it be love, gifts, goodness, understanding, or something else. Jesus sacrificed His life not because of what we could give to Him but because of His love for us. The flow will come back to you in another form.

An old friend called my husband and I twenty years ago to ask if she could borrow $350, which was a lot of money to us then, as we were raising a young family. I respected what my husband told her. He said, "We will *give* you $250. You do not have to pay it back." He offered an amount that we could be comfortable with giving away so that there would be no hard feelings on our part if our friend never paid back the money. This freed her up as well, from feelings of indebtedness to us. As it turned out, she paid us back, down to the last penny and more, but that was her choice. In this case, the flow came back to us from her.

One young lady told me that she had been practicing speaking more positively to her husband but had received nothing back from him. Was she giving while expecting something in return? Give, and be comforted in the thought that what goes around might come around from a different source. Your giving will not go unrewarded, but do not give for that reason. Usually, when you stop expecting reciprocation from your spouse is when things begin to change for the better.

If you are following your lightness or your inner guidance, then doors will open up and you will flow. Sometimes we make a decision based on pure logic when the thing we are choosing may not be right for us. Then we are surprised when things are not working out even though the math made sense.

What are we not willing to put back into circulation that is taking the place of something new and better? What is the treasure that we are holding onto that no longer serves us and that, in fact, hinders us from getting something more or different?

Jesus said in Matthew 6:19, "Lay not up for yourselves treasures upon earth, where moth and rust doth corrupt, and where thieves break through and steal."

When our focus is on accumulating things or material "treasures," we are actually robbed of opportunities for increasing our faith and abundance. As you release, you create the space for the new, for possibilities, and for fresh new experiences to come to you.

The higher your faith, the more you will feel free to give and receive, and to clean the closets of your life on all

Law of Circulation (Flow)

planes. You will be opening the floodgates that contribute mightily to this flow.

Flow of Forgiveness

Matthew 18 tells us about a king whose servant owed him ten thousand talents (currency of that day). The servant fell down, worshipped his king, and begged for patience. The king was moved with compassion and forgave the servant his debt.

This same servant then went to demand payment from a fellow servant who owed him far less. This other servant begged for patience, but the first servant refused the request and cast his debtor into prison until he could pay his debt in full.

When the king heard about this, he became angry.

Jesus said the following in Matthew 18:32–35:

> Then his lord, after that he had called him, said unto him, O thou wicked servant, I forgave thee all that debt, because thou desiredst me: Shouldest not thou also have had compassion on thy fellow servant, even as I had pity on thee? And his lord was wroth, and delivered him to the tormentors, till he should pay all that was due unto him. So likewise shall my

heavenly Father do also unto you, if ye from your hearts forgive not every one his brother their trespasses.

So where did the flow stop? The wicked servant received the flow of forgiveness from his king, but then he stopped it when he would not take that same forgiveness and pass it on to his fellow servant. As a result, the flow turned negative, and he was put in prison himself.

By forgiving another, we are actually freeing ourselves from negative flow. Any hardness you have for anyone will hinder your own flow of abundance.

Flow of Grace

Grace is God's unearned favor and power. It is free, but it cannot be earned and it is not deserved. It is received as a gift by faith, not merited by works.

John 1:16 reads, "And of his fullness have all we received, and grace for grace."

This flow of grace became available to all of humanity at the time of Jesus's death; however, this grace can only be accessed by faith. We can parallel this principle to a water hose and water. The water is like the grace of God, available in abundance. Faith is like the water hose that gives us access to the flow of water so we can benefit from it. We cannot access the grace of God without faith. As it says in Ephesians 2:8–9, *"For by grace are ye saved through faith*; and that not of yourselves: it is the gift of God: Not of works, lest any man should boast".

Grace covers those with faith who come short of the mark; it fills the gap. Example: If you are in a race, cannot go any farther, and fall ten meters from the finish line, then grace would cover that gap, in a spiritual sense. However, grace would not cover someone who did not have the faith to even begin the race.

We live in a world of earning, deserving, and merit, and these things all result in judgment, which hinders flow. Grace allows us to maintain flow in our lives through faith. It is the unmerited power and favor that God gives to those who believe. The grace of God is about believing and receiving, not about earning and deserving.

As we receive this grace from God, we no longer wish to hoard all the goodness we receive. Rather, we continue the flow and share the goodness to help others in their time of need.

Hebrews 4:16 reads, "Let us therefore come boldly unto the throne of grace, that we may obtain mercy, and find grace to help in time of need."

Law of Circulation (Flow)

Flow of Mercy

Mercy is about showing compassion and kindness toward someone whom it is within our power to punish or harm.

I thought of a heartwarming World War II story of mercy. Two American fighter pilots were cruising through German airspace when they saw a grey German Messerschmitt fighter hovering just three feet from one of their wingtips. It was five days before Christmas 1943, and the fighter had closed in on their crippled American B-17 bomber for the kill. The B-17 pilot, Charles Brown, was a twenty-one-year-old West Virginia farm boy on his first combat mission. When Brown and his copilot made eye contact with the German fighter pilot, something odd happened. The German did not pull the trigger. He nodded at Brown instead. This was one of the most remarkable acts of chivalry and mercy recorded during World War II. Years later, Brown would track down his would-be executioner for a reunion that reduced both men to tears.

I also thought of a mother who pleaded with the judge to show mercy for her son at his trial. The judge told her that her son did not deserve his mercy. She said, "Your Honor, if he did deserve it, then it would not be mercy but justice."

Mercy from God is something that none of us deserve, yet God rains his mercy upon everyone.

Matthew 5:45 reads, "That ye may be the children of your Father which is in heaven: for he maketh his sun to rise on the evil and on the good, and sendeth *rain* on the just and on the unjust".

We read throughout the Old Testament of the many times when God showed mercy to the Israelites. Time and time again, they turned their back on Him, yet He gave them another day of mercy and another opportunity. Moses interceded many times for the people. Many people today do not even give a thought toward God. Some deny His existence, yet He continues to give them oxygen to breathe, warmth from the sunshine, food to eat, and water to drink. God is merciful and kind. However, His mercy might run out one day.

Romans 9:15 reads, "For he saith to Moses, I will have mercy on whom I will have mercy, and I will have compassion on whom I will have compassion."

God will decide whether or not to be merciful toward us. Mercy is a gift, not something we expect or deserve.

Mercy and grace are often associated with each other. Paul had reason to expect punishment or harsh treatment because of his zealous persecution of the early Christians, as recorded in Acts 8. Instead, he received unexpected benevolence and forgiveness. He himself was called to be

Law of Circulation (Flow)

a Christian minister of the Gospel. That mercy, however, did not forgive his sins or justify him before God. Paul was justified by grace—through faith. Jesus can only cover our sins as much as we believe He can. If we do not believe, then we face our Creator on our own, baggage and all. What does it mean to turn from our ways and believe? Tune in to your inner guidance team with gratitude, verbally ask (or give thanks) for guidance, and then be patient. It may take time for events to be divinely arranged to align with your request. Then follow your peace and inspirations that come. Ask and you shall receive.

Jesus said in Matthew 5:7, "Blessed are the merciful: for they shall obtain mercy."

His mercy will continue to flow to us as we show mercy to others. Mercy is often tied to the concept of forgiveness. For instance, an act of mercy would be forgiving or releasing someone who has wronged or hurt you. The higher your level of faith, the more mercy you might show to others. A lack of forgiveness or hardness of heart cannot exist in a space of love.

King Solomon wrote in Proverbs 14:21, "He who despiseth his neighbor sinneth; but he that hath mercy on the poor, happy is he."

Showing mercy to others breeds happiness within us. Happy are we as we allow the mercy of God to flow through us to others.

Law of Circulation (Flow)

Be Sensitive to Your Flowmeter

Whatever you feel you are lacking in this life is what you need to give (love, understanding, money, time, etc.). If one day you are feeling short on funds, then that is the day you might want to go out and buy someone a cup of coffee. If you are putting money in a parking meter and only fifteen minutes is required, then put in a toonie, or a $2 coin. Let someone else benefit from the money you fed the meter. Flow will begin again when you have this mindset. Similarly, if you feel that you are not being understood, then you need to seek to understand.

Where are you stuck? What are you not willing to let go of that which is no longer serving you? Are you stuck in the area of relationships? This is not about letting go of the relationship itself. It is more about looking inward. Perhaps you are not letting go of a grudge against your loved one. Perhaps there is a lack of self-respect and honor, and you are leaving a lot of love on the table because of your feelings of unworthiness. Let go of the very thing that is blocking you from flowing.

You will know something is not quite right if doors seem to close on you. If you continually encounter roadblocks, then double check your position. Maybe you are heading down a wrong path or holding onto something you need to let go of.

Law of Circulation (Flow)

The first time a roadblock comes up, take notice. If it appears again and again, then rethink a decision. This could be a guide for making a business decision, taking a vacation, applying at a school, or dealing with matters of the heart. Let us take applying at a school as an example. What happens if the school of your choice rejects you? Do you hold on to disappointment? Release it. Let it go. Move on. If you were meant to attend there, the door would have opened up. If you fight the rejection and finally get accepted, then your time at that school will not be as smooth for you as another path would have been. It is one thing to put forth time and effort into something that we are inspired and passionate about, as long as it still feels right and light. However, if we keep hitting roadblocks, then perhaps we are on the wrong path.

In Numbers 22, we read about the prophet Balaam who was approached by Balak, King of the Moabites. The king wanted Balaam to put a curse on the Israelites because he was afraid that they would take over the land, so he bribed him with money. Balaam agreed. As Balaam was heading out on his donkey to do the deed, an angel of the Lord stood in front of him to stop him. Balaam directed his donkey around the angel, went into a field, and continued on his way. The angel appeared a second time to Balaam on a vineyard path by a wall. This time the donkey thrust herself into the wall, crushing Balaam's foot. He still continued on. The angel appeared a third time in front of Balaam, only this time it was in a narrow place where he could not go to the right or the left. The donkey fell to its knees and refused to move.

Numbers 22:31–34 reads as follows:

> Then the Lord opened the eyes of Balaam, and he saw the angel of the Lord standing in the way, and his sword drawn in his hand: and he bowed down his head, and fell flat on his face. And the angel of the Lord said unto him, Wherefore hast thou smitten thine ass these three times? behold, I went out to withstand thee, because thy way is perverse before me: And the ass saw me, and turned from me these three times: unless she had turned from me, surely now also I had slain thee, and saved her alive. And Balaam said unto the angel of the Lord, I have sinned; for I knew not that thou stoodest in the way against me: now therefore, if it displease thee, I will get me back again.

If Balaam had been sensitive to his inner guidance, then he would have known that he was doing the wrong thing the first time the angel stopped him. The first time the angel appeared, it was a light warning. The second time

Law of Circulation (Flow)

was more severe. After the third warning, Balaam was stopped in his tracks. How many warnings do we need before we catch on to the fact that we are out of flow? It would be wonderful if we took heed to the first feather warning us that we were off track. If we do not take heed, then perhaps the next time will be a brick warning, a little more obvious and severe. Or do we want to continue on until we are forced to be stopped in our tracks?

You are in vibration resonance with abundance through your physical acts of maintaining flow on all three planes in your life. Remember, nothing in this world belongs to us. We will take nothing with us when we die, so we must not hold any attachments. You proclaim that everything you have belongs to God when you give away a portion of it.

Chapter 6

LAW OF ABUNDANCE

The law of abundance states that the universe is filled to abundance with everything we need to live and thrive. There is an abundance of life everywhere around us, from our forests to vegetation to oceans to all life forms, including little creatures and humankind alike. Our universe was created in such a way that abundance and plenty is all there is.

Grass, like everything in creation, begins as a seed. It begins to sprout with the abundant supply of sunshine, water, and nutrients provided to it. As it grows and matures, it begins to produce additional seeds. This self-sustaining cycle continues and is repeated season after season, year after year, century after century.

The entire universe is continually operating in its unwavering and unfailing fashion. It knows no such thing as lack and limitation. As you take a breath of air into your lungs, or take a bucketful of water out of the ocean, abundance remains. Your abundance or your experience of abundance in no way removes or takes away from anyone else's abundance.

A verse in the Upanishads reads, "From abundance he took abundance, and still abundance remains."

We make room for abundance in our lives when we create space for it. We create space in our lives by letting go of things that no longer serve us, or by giving to others and continuing the flow. Abundance exists not only in the physical world, which we observe with our five senses, but also on the unseen mental and spiritual planes. We live in a universe where we create our world with our thoughts. The quality of our thoughts (seeds) and consciousness determines what we receive an abundance of. Abundance is based on what is happening internally. It manifests itself externally. If we think limiting thoughts of lack, then that is what will be brought into our physical world. However, the universe is abundant and the law of abundance states that abundance is everywhere and for everyone.

We are always abundant in something, even if it is an abundance of lack and limitation. Having a healthy abundance on the lower plane means you are able to do what you need to do when you need to do it. Relax the need to think that abundance has to come in a certain way. Otherwise, you close all other doors through which it could come because you have set an expectation. The universe cannot give to us beyond what we have concluded. Let abundance come along the path of least resistance. There is enough for everyone. You do not have to make it work. All you have to do is to allow it to work, because it already works.

The law of abundance states that the universe is willing to support us unconditionally in our belief about ourselves. If you believe that you are a person who is bad, worthless, and a failure, then the universe will support you unconditionally in that belief and will give you more of that same energy, which will attract more of the same negative thoughts and experiences. If it is willing to support you when you say you are hateful, worthless, and undeserving, then it is certainly willing to support you when you say that you are creative, loving, and deserving. When you decide what is true for you, the universe will not contradict you. It will simply reflect whatever you have said is true about you at that moment. You have free will to decide, through your thoughts and spoken words, who and what you are. That reflection is given to you through your passion and excitement.[1]

Abundance within the universe has always been here, and it will always be here as long as it exists. There is no more electricity in the world today than there was one

---

[1] For more on this, watch the video here: https://www.youtube.com/watch?v=UkwU-A6aSSw.

hundred years ago. It was not until someone recognized the law by which electricity could be made to serve that we received benefit. Now that the law is understood, practically the whole world uses electricity. It is only those who recognize the law of abundance and place themselves in harmony with it who are the ones to share in its benefits. It is good for us to remember that no more effort is required to aim high in life and achieve abundance and prosperity than is required to accept misery and poverty. The law of abundance is based on our beliefs about ourselves.

The fact that most people do not see abundance around them is evidence that they do not understand, or do not apply, the law. In their blindness, they say that plenty does not exist for them, and as far as they can see, they may be right. It is only as we rise in consciousness that our belief about ourselves can change.

The formula for abundance: combine a clear intention with an elevated feeling or belief that you have already been granted your request. We cannot think greater than how we feel. Teach your body what the future is going to feel like before the future is made manifest. The event will soon catch up with you. We do not wait for wealth to show up to feel abundance. We do not wait for success to feel empowerment. We do not wait for healing to feel wholeness. We do not wait for a new relationship to feel love. Create the feeling or belief first, along with intention.

When we do this, we are changing the brain and body on a biological level. The end result organizes events in our life that are equal to that state of being. We do not pray to have our prayers answered. With faith, we get up from prayer as if our prayer is already answered. [2]

It is the same with everything else. Once you create thoughts of abundance and believe those thoughts, abundance will appear in your life everywhere. We can be proactive and create our physical world from thoughts on the mental plane. Whatever you create in your thoughts will manifest itself as you set a clear intention with no ego attachments, believe it has already happened, and get on with your day.

Where do you fit on the chart below?

Abundance Mentality	Scarcity or Lack Mentality
Grateful	Ungrateful
Celebrates when others do well	Is jealous of others
Accepting; looks for good in others	Is judgmental of others
Generous	Sparing
Trust-based decision making	Fear-based decision making
Inspires and energizes people	Depletes the energy of others
Treats everyone with respect	Believes he or she is better than some
Focus is on others	Focus is on self
Open-minded and flexible	Closed-minded, rigid, restricted
Sees abundance around them	Sees lack around them
Lives in the present moment	Often distracted
Embraces life	Timid, fearful
"How may I serve today?"	"What's in it for me?"

---

[2] Dr. Joe Dispenza, Neurosummit III, 2015.

Does the state of the economy dictate our abundance? I live in a province where oil and gas are the mainstay. The current price of crude oil today is $37.35 per barrel, down from $136.31 seven years ago. People are panicking. Thousands of people have lost their jobs. How does this affect people who have a lack mentality? They may feel justified in living a life in misery and lack. How does this economy affect people with an abundance mentality? They understand that there is just as much abundance in the world today as there was before the price of oil dropped. The abundance has just shifted.

Ask empowering questions, see what new opportunities show up, and act on inspirations that come.

Law of Abundance (Bible)

Job knew abundance in his life on all levels. He had a large family, wealth, power, influence, health, and faith in God. When his wealth, family, and health were taken from him, his faith in God remained intact. His belief system was not shattered, even though others around him tried to get him to curse God.

Job 1:22 reads, "In all this Job sinned not, nor charged God foolishly."

It was because of his strong faith in God that abundance was brought back to him again.

Law of Abundance

Job 42:10, 12 reads, "And the Lord turned the captivity of Job, when he prayed for his friends: also the Lord gave Job twice as much as he had before. … So the Lord blessed the latter end of Job more than his beginning."

I love that Job's flow of abundance began again when he was finally able to pray for his misguided friends and look beyond himself. His abundance did not just come in the form of physical wealth, a new family, and health. It came on all levels. He was richer in all areas of his life.

It says in Job 42:5, "I have heard of thee by the hearing of the ear: but now mine eye seeth thee."

His relationship with God was strengthened as a result of this experience. He knew God at a deeper level, as he had seen and experienced His work firsthand.

What is the correlation of faith and abundance for us today? Jesus said in John 10:10, "I am come that they might have life, and that they might have it more abundantly." Was Jesus referring to abundant "spiritual" life? We now know that what affects one plane affects the other two. If we are abundant with the fruit of the Spirit, such as peace, joy, and love, then this will affect us on the mental and physical planes. This fruit will affect all sides of our life. I like to think that God intended that we would all live an abundant life as we depend on His love. However, it might take many tough experiences before we get there. What if we were to welcome each experience that causes

Law of Abundance

us to dig deep and increases our faith? If cancer or sickness comes upon us, maybe we ought not to think of it as a lack of abundance and become discouraged. Rather, let us look at it as a gift, because it is an opportunity for us to grow in faith, which will then add to our abundance. Every experience, good or bad, has the potential to add to our abundance.

Jesus says in Matthew 7:7, "Ask, and it shall be given you; seek, and ye shall find; knock, and it shall be opened unto you."

There is no lack. If we feel we are lacking, then we are not asking. What is abundance? Abundance to God is all things. I do not believe He differentiates between love, wealth, fellowship, grace, goodness, etc. Abundance is a high-vibrating faith or energy. The higher our faith, the more of this abundance we will attract on all planes and in all areas of our life.

In Matthew 25, we read of the man who gave his three servants talents (currency of that time). He gave five talents to one servant, two talents to another servant, and one talent to a third servant. The first two doubled their money, and the last one buried his talent, so he did not have an increase. The flow stopped with the man who hoarded and buried his talent. The first two circulated what they were given and they received an increase. The third man had a lack mentality, so abundance remained elusive to him.

God understands that we need to provide for our families. There is more than enough for all of us. Matthew 6:31–34 reads as follows:

> Therefore take no thought, saying, What shall we eat? or, What shall we drink? or, Wherewithal shall we be clothed? (For after all these things do the Gentiles seek:) for your heavenly Father knoweth that ye have need of all these things. But seek ye first the kingdom of God, and his righteousness; and all these things shall be added unto you. Take therefore no thought for the morrow: for the morrow shall take thought for the things of itself.

As Jesus clearly states, if we put the kingdom of God (which is within us) first in faith and trust, then things will work out on the lower planes.

Jesus says in Matthew 6:26, "Behold the fowls of the air: for they sow not, neither do they reap, nor gather into barns; yet your heavenly Father feedeth them. Are ye not much better than they."

There is a difference between a godly sense of responsibility and an ungodly, untrusting worry. However, an ungodly, untrusting sense of worry can sometimes masquerade as responsibility. God provides for the birds, but they do not just sit with open mouths, expecting God to feed them. The birds do not worry and stress over where their next meal will come from. They just go out and get it. They are up early every day gathering their food and feeding their young.

This law of abundance may be a difficult thing to absorb. Many Christians believe that God does not care about the natural side of our life, especially our financial concerns. None of us know with certainty what God thinks. All we know for sure is that *His thoughts are way above our thoughts.* This is why it helps us to understand the laws of the universe, because they give us a little glimpse into the mind of our Creator. When you ask God with faith for help to come your way so you can pay your outstanding bills, I do not believe that He is visualizing paper money. Rather, I believe God is picking up on the level of faith that you have attached to your request. If you ask believing that you have already received it (as Jesus stated in Mark 11:24), then God will give you more of that same energy back, meaning that you attract the help on your own. Say that two people ask for the same thing. One asks in belief that he already has received it, and the other asks with doubt. God, in His loving-kindness, has answered both petitions according to their faith. Only one person has manifested what he asked for.

Faith is mentioned 336 times in the Bible, 280 of those mentions appearing in the New Testament. Faith is not an option when it comes to obtaining abundance. As we learn how to flow with the laws on the lower planes, we gain great potential for abundance on the spiritual plane.

Paul says the following in 2 Corinthians 9:6:

> But this I say, He which soweth sparingly shall reap also sparingly; and he which soweth bountifully shall reap also bountifully. Every man according as he purposeth in his heart, so let him give; not grudgingly, or of necessity: for God loveth a cheerful giver. And God is able to make all grace abound toward you; that ye, always having all sufficiency in all things, may abound to every good work: (As it is written, He hath dispersed abroad; he hath given to the poor: his righteousness remaineth for ever.

Abundance comes as we let go of attachments and pass on a portion of what we have onto others, thereby making room for more abundance. When we get caught up in materialism, it becomes a low-vibration attachment and hinders our flow. To clarify, wealth is not the root of all evil, but rather the *love* of it is. It is when we attach emotion to wealth, whether greed or neediness, that our flow stops and we become stuck in that area.

Paul says in 1 Timothy 6:10, "For the *love* of money is the root of all evil: which while some coveted after, they have erred from the faith, and pierced themselves through with many sorrows".

We might think that it a no-brainer that some of the wealthiest people are the greatest philanthropists. What came first, though: the giving or the wealth? If we look at Warren Buffett, American business magnate, we read that he has given a portion of his earnings away to those less fortunate all his life. He did not wait until he had millions or billions. I must clarify again that we should never give with the selfish motive of receiving back tenfold. Our motive must be cheerful, selfless giving in order for abundance to flow.

Is it possible to be abundant in faith on the spiritual plane but to have a lack of faith in certain areas of the lower planes? For example, is it possible to have a strong love *for* God, yet struggle financially? Yes. I call these faith blocks. There might be a lack of faith or belief in that one area. When we are *struggling* financially, there are usually negative feelings of lack attached, which create a block. Because of your past experiences, you might feel that you are not capable of having any more abundance in that area. You will not, as long as that is your belief. Again, it is the negative emotions that create the block, not the fact of having little money. Some folks choose less and are very happy and content. If we had *perfect* faith, then we would be dwelling within the *perfect* love of God, where there are no feelings of lack or limitations on any level. We know that *perfect* love casts out fear and other low-vibrating frequencies. It is impossible for love and fear to dwell together. Only Jesus knew perfection, so faith blocks are something the rest of us struggle with. One by one, we hope to overcome these limiting faith blocks so we can abide in perfect love and faith.

On the other hand, is it possible to be financially wealthy yet not have faith in God or a higher power? Yes. Because we are what we believe we are, we attract like vibrations back to us in whatever relevant area of our life. A person could have high belief in one area and not be abundant in other areas. Her lack of faith in a higher power will definitely limit her in life or keep her from reaching her full potential overall. We have often heard of those who come across wealth overnight, like lottery winners or beneficiaries of an estate. Often, these people are not able to hold onto their windfall because their deep-rooted beliefs about themselves do not have sufficient time to change before the money is spent.

Remember the law about flow. If we have a financial faith block, then perhaps the first thing we ought to do is stop hoarding and start giving more—that is, loosen our attachment to money. If you focus on the higher plane (the ways to increase your faith, as discussed) and refrain from placing any emotional attachment on that block on the lower planes, then all the faith blocks you have will eventually lift to allow flow. It is when you attach ego emotion (greed or neediness) to what you desire that you become stuck. Attachment will always stop the flow. Belief is the seed. The law of abundance produces an abundance of whatever you choose to believe (i.e., whatever you plant). That is what determines the kind and quality of your thoughts, emotions, and reactions in life.

King Solomon wrote in Proverbs 23:7, "For as he thinketh in his heart, so is he."

We are who we believe we are. The law of abundance produces an abundance of whatever we choose to think about and focus on most, positive or negative.

In my own work with others, I find that lack of self-worth seems to be the most common abundance block that hinders faith and spiritual growth. Perhaps this block stems from negative childhood experiences, current negative living situations, or even religious beliefs stipulating that it is not right to love and honor yourself. When Jesus talks about denying ourselves in Matthew 16:24, I believe He is referring to denying the ego, or our human nature, and then following our inner guidance system. When we follow our inner guidance team, it is not drudgery but is lightness and liberation. When we follow our ego strictly, it might take us to places that may satisfy our ego for a short time, but then heaviness develops within us due to low vibration activities. The more we become in tune to our own "gut energy," the more we can feel the difference between the two guidance systems.

I love the picture of God's abundance and provision in Psalms 23. David expresses it as follows:

> The Lord is my shepherd; I shall not want. He maketh me to lie down in green pastures: he leadeth me beside the still waters. He restoreth my soul: he leadeth me in the paths of righteousness for his name's sake. Yea, though I walk through the valley of the shadow of death, I will fear no evil: for thou art with me; thy rod and thy staff they comfort me. Thou preparest a table before me in the presence of mine enemies: thou anointest my head with oil; my cup runneth over. Surely goodness and mercy shall follow me all the days of my life: and I will dwell in the house of the Lord for ever.

This is a beautiful picture of the abundance that can be ours when we trust in that which is greater than ourselves. Our once empty cup of life can be filled to overflowing with goodness, even in the presence of our enemies (ego limitations). If God were to pour blessings into your cup in proportion to your faith, how full would your cup be? If you are living a contented, happy, but faithless life, your cup at best could only be half full based on the law of vibration, which requires belief or faith to better our existence on the lower planes. Just think of the rich potential of extra blessings you would experience on top of your contentment if you added faith to that mix.

Summary

The following things stop the flow of abundance:

1. Judgment of ourselves or others
2. Not being balanced in giving and receiving
3. Having feelings of unworthiness (This will stop of the flow of God's abundance because it indicates self-focus or self-judgment, which limits God, because He cannot give us more than we feel worthy of.)
4. Lack of belief or faith (Remember, God cannot give us more than our belief system will allow on all three planes.)
5. Dishonesty—with ourselves, others, and God

6. Hoarding or materialism; stashing away money for ourselves and not paying bills or taxes, and not giving a portion to others (or to the church or a charity that means something to you)
7. Fear (Do not settle. When you refuse to play small and you take a risk by opening yourself up, with the intention of receiving more in your life, what you are doing is nourishing that part of you that magnetizes the good stuff and keeps the flow going.)

Exercise: In a quiet moment, open your heart and arms and say verbally to God, "Dear Father, I am open to receiving whatever gift of abundance You want to give to me today. I will accept it with joy and gratitude."

Keep in mind that what God may want to give you could be as simple as a gift or a phone call from someone else just at the right time. Feel your heart open up to receive it with gratitude. See what shows up in your day, having no expectations. The above prayer might be something you want to say every morning. Then, when something wonderful shows up in your day, perhaps an unexpected visitor, a beautiful sunset, or even a beautiful butterfly that passes by, give thanks to God. He will send you exactly what you need.

Chapter 7

LAW OF CAUSE AND EFFECT

The law of cause and effect states that every cause has an effect and every effect becomes the cause of something else. This law suggests that the universe is always in motion and progresses from a chain of events.[1]

Nothing happens in isolation. Every event can be traced to one or more events that preceded it and that, in fact, *caused* it. We might ask the following questions: "How did this happen?" "What caused this?" "Where did this come from?" "When did it start?" Or, more incisively, "Why did this happen?"

Police investigators on an accident scene, for instance, use the principle of cause and effect every day to determine who was ultimately responsible and how it happened.

---

[1] For more information on the law of cause and effect, visit http://lawsoftheuniverse.weebly.com/law-of-cause-and-effect.html.

When we try to trace the event to its cause or causes, we find that we never seem to reach a stopping point. The cause of the event was itself caused by a prior cause, which was affected by a previous cause, and so on. Eventually the event would be traced back to the original cause of existence: the God of creation.

Life does not happen *to* us. Life happens *through* us and *as* us, and we are at cause. Nothing can come into our life unless it comes out of us first being activated by our consciousness on some level. The world cannot add anything to us, but it also cannot take anything away. All it can be is a canvas on which we paint our masterpiece, or a mirror within which we get feedback. Of itself, our world around us is just a projection of our own perception.[2]

What does this mean for us today? As we are created in the image of God and have freewill choice over our own reality in this realm, everything that happens to us in our world can be traced back to the first cause: the creation of our own world by us. All that happens in my life, for example, can be traced back to my inner world of thoughts and beliefs.

Every human thought, word, and deed is a cause that sets off a wave of energy throughout the universe, which in turn manifests the effect, whether desirable or undesirable. With every thought of intention, action, and emotion

---

[2] See http://len.life/shows/the-aware-show/derek-rydall.

that is transmitted from you, an unseen chain of effects is set into motion, which vibrates from the mental plane of consciousness through the entire cellular structure of the body, moves out into the environment, and finally moves into the universe. That energy is attracted back to you and manifested into your reality.

Law of Cause and Effect (Bible)

Jesus says in Luke 6:38, "*Give, and it shall be given unto you*; good measure, pressed down, and shaken together, and running over, shall men give into your bosom. *For with the same measure that ye mete withal it shall be measured to you again*".

Paul said in Galatians 6:7–8, "Be not deceived; God is not mocked: *for whatsoever a man soweth, that shall he also reap*. For he that soweth to his flesh shall of the flesh reap corruption; but he that soweth to the Spirit shall of the Spirit reap life everlasting".

"For whatsoever a man soweth, that shall he also reap." There do not seem to be any victims here. Are we *all* responsible for what happens to us? What about the unfortunate among us who fall prey to others? Whether or not you feel like you had control over negative experiences in the past, if you were to trace back the chain of events, you would see that the reality is that you are *now* responsible for your life from this day forward. What are you going to sow today that will give you the results you want for the future?

My paternal grandfather was a man of high faith and integrity. He was raised in small-town Manitoba by a father who was a drunkard, and his brother eventually became a drunkard as well. Someone asked his brother, "Why are you wasting your life like this, living off the bottle?" His response was, "What do you expect? Have you met my father?" This same man asked my grandfather, "How come you don't drink?" My grandfather replied, "Have you ever met my father? If you have, then you will know why I don't drink!" Two people can come out of the same tough childhood, and one of them can use that difficult experience as power to propel him forward in life to greater things, whereas the other might choose to use that experience as a crutch to justify a life of misery or anger.

If we follow our conscience and are led by our divine team to higher consciousness and faith, then we will reap goodness in our lives now and forever. This does not mean that we will not go through times of sorrow, distress, or illness. Rather, we will reap goodness *in or from* these tough experiences.

Again, let us look at the life of Job. He was a blameless and an upright man, so why did he go through the devastating experience of having all he cared about taken away from

Law of Cause and Effect

him? If we reap what we sow, then what was the cause for Job to experience this traumatic effect?

Job 2:3 reads, "And the Lord said unto Satan, Hast thou considered my servant Job, that there is none like him in the earth, a perfect and an upright man, one that feareth God, and escheweth evil? and still he holdeth fast his integrity, although thou movedst me against him, to destroy him without cause."

Job had sown faith and trust in God before this experience. Therefore, he reaped bountifully as a result of this experience. It was evident by the fruit produced what he had sown. The experience itself may not always be an effect, but it will deliver the effect. We may not choose the experience, but if we have sown the right things into our life, then we will harvest more of the same. Every experience, good or bad, can enrich us. God can use situations that we might have no power over as an opportunity to add to our purpose and abundance. We know that Job gained much more at the end of this experience than what he had started out with. Before, he knew God from a distance.

I believe that God knew Job's potential and that He allowed him to be tested by Satan so that greater purpose and enrichment could be brought into his life.

When we think of the tough experiences we went through in the past, let us determine to use those situations to propel us forward in life in a positive way that enriches us and causes us to dig deep within ourselves, which will take us to a higher vibration and greater faith. Any experience that causes us to turn to our Creator will not be in vain. However, if we allow these experiences to harden us to a lower vibration level, we will only attract more of these same low-level situations into our lives, making the initial experience be all for naught.

In Matthew 13, Jesus talks about the kingdom of heaven as being like a man who sowed good seed in his field. While the farmer slept, his enemy came in, sowed tares (weeds) among the wheat, and then went on his way. The farmer did not discover this until the blades were up.

Jesus says the following in Matthew 13:26–30:

> But when the blade was sprung up, and brought forth fruit, then appeared the tares also. So the servants of the householder came and said unto him, Sir, didst not thou sow good seed in thy field? from whence then hath it tares? He said unto them, An enemy hath done this. The servants said unto him, Wilt thou then that we go and gather them up? But he said, Nay; lest while ye gather up the tares, ye root up also the wheat with them. Let both grow together until the harvest: and in the time of harvest I

> will say to the reapers, Gather ye together first the tares, and bind them in bundles to burn them: but gather the wheat into my barn.

It was beyond the farmer's control that someone else had put weeds in his crop while he slept. The farmer took this unplanned seemingly negative situation and flowed with it. He separated the weeds from the crop at harvest, instead of reacting at the time, which could have harmed the wheat.

Sometimes weeds are okay. Under controlled circumstances, a number of beneficial weeds can help our gardens. They hold topsoil, pull up water and nutrients, provide food, help control insects, and more. Can we flow in an unfavorable situation and use it in a positive way that will enrich us and benefit us in the long term?

In conclusion, in order for the law of cause and effect to benefit us and society as a whole on the lower planes of consciousness, we ought to use our freewill choice and perform good deeds with the awareness in mind that what we think, act on, and speak about (cause) will affect our world around us. As we move into the higher spiritual plane of consciousness, we will reap and enjoy the fruit of the Spirit and learn how to sow in even greater faith.

Chapter 8

LAW OF DETACHMENT

The law of detachment states that the way to acquire anything in this universe is to relinquish our attachment to it. This does not mean that we give up on goal setting or setting an intention, but rather that we release our emotional attachment to the goal or the end result.[1] By not attaching emotion to the way in which our request or intention will materialize, we remain open to new possibilities and inspirations that might show up along the way that bring about actualization. When we combine an intention with detachment, then what is best for us will show up. It may be what we ask for, or it may be something better. Either way, it will be best for us.

When we do not judge one potential end result as being greater than another, our intention has a greater chance of being realized. When every choice is equal with neutral

---

[1] For more information, see http://www.amberallen.com/personal-growth/law-detachment/.

emotion, then we will receive what is in our best interest. When we become emotionally attached to a particular outcome, then we may repel the very thing we are trying to attract, as desperate energy attracts desperate situations. Example: If we really *need* that job we are applying for, then our needy or desperate energy will attract desperate circumstances. However, if we remain neutral, then we will attract the position if it is in our best interests. If we focus on what we do not want (getting into an accident, having a lack of money, getting cancer), then we only attract more of these experiences into our lives by default, that is, through our fearful energy. Whenever we make something stand out, positive or negative, we are putting energy into it and saying that it needs to be greater than anything else. We might be using all the right words by desiring a specific outcome, but our desperate energy might be repelling the very thing we are trying to attract or make happen.

Attachment is based on fear and insecurity. The search for security indicates an attachment to our *known* past experiences and past conditioning. When we relinquish emotion to the known, we open ourselves up to unlimited possibilities, inviting creativity and inspiration. Many of us look for happiness and security outside of ourselves. When we truly understand that our divine team knows best and that all the answers are within us, we begin to understand that we do not need anything outside of ourselves to make us happy. We know that whatever is on the outside that brings us happiness has the same potential to bring us pain if it is taken away. The only way of escaping this dilemma is to become detached. One way of accomplishing this is to set intentions with a spirit of playfulness. "If my intention works out, great! If it doesn't, then that is great, too! If I don't receive it, then that is what must be best for me!" Have some fun with it!

Our youngest son was at a corporate golf tournament one summer. When it came time to hand out the three door prizes after the BBQ supper, he threw the question out there into the unknown, "What would it take for my team to win two of the three prizes?" Sure enough, his twosome won two of the prizes. He was playful with it. It did not matter to him if he won or not, so he had no emotional attachment to the outcome. There was no desperate energy attached because he did not *need* to win. For the record, I did reprimand him for this selfish ego request, even though I knew he was just testing the system. It is important to be mindful of whether we are asking for something from a place of ego or from a place of rightness, of what is best for us (soul guidance). If we are asking from a place of ego, then our request could *bring leanness to our soul* and will not contribute to our overall purpose. In fact, it could hinder us from carrying out our purpose. Using this law is not a matter of using God to get more stuff in the world. Rather, it is about using everything in the world to get us closer to God. As Jesus said, "But seek ye first the kingdom of God, and his righteousness; and all these things shall be added unto you" (Matthew 6:33).

We often hear people say that they need this or they need that. They need this to happen in a relationship, or they really need that job. This vibration is suggesting that they do not already have what they want, so their energy becomes needy, which will actually repel the very thing they want to attract.

The law of detachment is very much connected to the law of abundance. In fact, all universal laws flow together. Abundance on any level of consciousness comes when we relinquish the ego's emotional attachments to whatever it is we desire.

If we truly have the level of faith where we believe that we have already received what we desire (as Jesus made plain in Mark 11:24), then we will no longer desire it because we have it already. Therefore, there is no emotional attachment to our request. We ask (or thank) God for what we desire, believe with an energy or feeling that we have received it or know that it has been taken care of, and then get on with our day. This level of faith attracts what we believe we already are or have into our reality—or it brings something better. It is important to have total trust in the outcome, whatever that might be. What is best for us *will* show up when we ask for it in faith.

In my son's second year of college, one of his classes was a voluntary work-experience project with a start-up industry mentor who was trying to land a deal with a highly respected supplier. My son had made the arrangement for representatives from the two companies to meet for their first sales meeting. On the morning of the meeting, my son's industry mentor called to cancel the mentorship, citing unforeseen circumstances. This seemed like such a blow at the time, because my son would now have to find a new mentor and start the process all over again. Why did this not turn out as he had intended? As it turned out, he still went to the meeting without his mentor, and the supplier ended up becoming his mentor. The supplier was a top international company, from which my son gained valuable experience and received top marks. How does it get any better than that? Something far better showed up for him than what he had asked for. This is encouragement for you to trust the process.

Acceptance of the end result is the first step to detached involvement. Do not attach emotion to the hoped-for outcome. Treat all potential outcomes as equal, understanding that what is best for you will show up. This means that whenever you face a problem, you stay grounded in the wisdom of the unknown, while expectantly waiting for a solution to come forward. When we truly let go of trying to manipulate a situation or force a solution, then something greater than us responds. Doors of opportunity will then open up to something greater than we could ever have imagined. All we can do is marvel at the simplicity of the process.

Law of Detachment (Bible)

Colossians 3:1–2 reads, "If ye then be risen with Christ, seek those things which are above, where Christ sitteth on the right hand of God. *Set your affection on things above, not on things on the earth*". Here, Paul is reminding us not to become attached to the things on this earth, but rather to seek after the unseen things that truly do matter and will last forever. In Luke, Jesus tells us that the kingdom of God is within us, not in this external world.

Luke 17:20–21 reads, "And when he was demanded of the Pharisees, when the kingdom of God should come, he [Jesus] answered them and said, The kingdom of God cometh not with observation: Neither shall they say, Lo here! or, lo there! for, behold, *the kingdom of God is within you*".

James 4:2–3 reads, "Ye lust, and have not: ye kill, and desire to have, and cannot obtain: ye fight and war, *yet ye have not, because ye ask not. Ye ask, and receive not, because ye ask amiss, that ye may consume it upon your lusts"*. Why were these people not receiving what they desired? They forgot to ask. Or perhaps they did ask, but emotional lust was attached to their desire.

If it is not wise to attach emotions to our request to God, then what about attaching emotional need? Is neediness an emotional attachment? Does our weakness appeal to God?

Our weakness appeals to God as much as the neediness of a little one appeals to its tender parent. As that child grows, his or her needs are still prevalent, but trust has superseded needs. When a child wakes up in the morning, he does not stress and worry about how he will feed himself that day. The dependence on his parents for food, clothing, and shelter is there, but he has total trust that all will be taken care of. For the most part, it is a child's natural tendency to be playful, worry-free, and trusting. Even though a child has needs, the energy of neediness is not prevalent in the child when there is complete trust that his parent will provide. Our trust and faith in our Creator *must* supersede any feelings of neediness or weakness in order for our petition to be effective or for us to grow and expand in His love. In contrast, if our needy energy supersedes our trust or faith, then we will attract more of those same needy experiences into our lives. We know we need our God and Savior, but we have complete trust and faith in the provision of Jesus. God loves it when we turn to Him for help, *knowing* that all will be taken care of.

Remember, God picks up on the energy vibration of faith that we attach to our request. I have found it helpful to take the word *need* right out of my vocabulary, because it sends off an energy that suggests that I do not have what I am asking for, which is contrary to what Jesus taught in Mark 11:24. Neediness is an emotional energy of attachment belonging to the ego, not to the divine. This does not mean that we do not have needs, but rather that our faith has superseded those feelings of weaknesses. We are whole when we have complete faith in His love. The grace of God covers any weaknesses, or gaps.

We usually get to a low weak point in our experience that causes us to first turn to God and inquire of Him. We slowly build our trust and faith from there. We grow and become strong in His strength when we trust as a child trusts his parents. Jesus often used a child as an example in His teachings. He said in Matthew 18:4, "Whosoever therefore shall humble himself as this little child, the same is greatest in the kingdom of heaven."

A playful child lives in the present and is inspired by and delighted with everything around him. His mind is not wandering off to concerns created by the ego about abstract structures and conventions that adults have learned to worry about and become bound to. Children are naturally creative. In fact, every child is an artist until she is told that she is not. We can learn much from a child.

As children get older, parents are delighted to watch their growth and maturity. So it is with God. When we follow our inner guidance team, we become strong in His strength and wisdom as we come into being who we really are and find what our purpose is.

Afterword

One truth I hope you take away as a result of reading this book is the understanding that you are a creator, not a victim, of your world around you. We reap what we sow and attract experiences into our lives based on our own beliefs of who we think we are. "As a man thinketh in his heart, so is he" (Proverbs 23:7). It is our vibration frequency or level of faith that determines the things we attract into our life that will bring the potential to add abundance. If we wish to know a richer and more meaningful life, then we have the power to raise our faith or vibration accordingly.

Living in a state of gratitude could be the most powerful change you make that will have the most impact on your everyday life. It changes the way you look at a brother; it changes the way you view a situation or the world around you; it helps you to relinquish ego attachments to this earth, which frees you up to new and greater possibilities; it lifts you out of a dark and fearful place to lofty new heights; and it shifts your energy immediately to a higher frequency, which brings you closer to the love of our Creator. Once we truly understand the power of gratitude, it will affect every part of our lives. Gratitude immediately increases our faith, thereby increasing what we believe is possible.

Faith begins like a small grain of mustard seed—the seed of a mustard plant being the smallest among all herbs—that grows into a bush large enough for the birds to build nests on its branches. We do not need much faith to begin this process. Let us start with asking God (or thanking Him) for something small that we can easily believe will come to pass. As it becomes manifested or actualized, thank and give Him the glory and praise. Repeat the process. Thanking Him raises our vibration and faith even more, which allows us to become even bolder, yet respectful, in our petitions. Remember, we must learn to trust Him in the little things before we trust Him with our soul.

Jesus said in John 3:12, "I have spoken to you of earthly things and you do not believe; how then will you believe if I speak of heavenly things?"

My atheist niece said to me this spring, "Aunty, do not talk to me about faith. I want science." We researched and talked about vibration, energy, Einstein, Rutherford, and Bohr. What I found the most interesting and amazing was that everything I researched pointed back to God, because science is true when it acknowledges what God Himself has already defined and established from the beginning. When I think of Einstein's and Bohr's conclusions on subatomic particles, perhaps I can say in layperson's terms that these two scientists saw what they believed they saw, whether wave or particle. Is that not the beginning of faith? Do we believe what we see, or do we see what we believe? If science says that we are 99.9999 percent energy and 0.0001 percent physical substance, does this not suggest that we are so much more than physical beings living in a physical world?[2] If this is the case, then why do we place so much focus on that small percentage of the physical world? Is defining our present reality by what we perceive with our senses the biggest limitation we have?

Our son now seems to be living a helium-filled life these days, which is such a contrast to three years ago. Most days, he feels like he is literally floating through life. He told me the other day that he feels like he walks around with God's hand on his shoulder leading him forward to greater and grander views. Every day, he is amazed at what shows up. Whatever he lacks, he receives because he believes. Whenever he finds himself running short on college funds, he sends out intention to receive more. Almost every time, an email or phone call will come within a day or two announcing that he was just awarded a scholarship or bursary. He would not have had opportunity to receive these funds had he not acted on his

---

[2] Dr. Joe Dispenza, *Breaking the Habit of Being Yourself* – Hay House (2012) Notes, 315

earlier inspirations to apply for these scholarships. So it is with us. Let us move forward in faith, act on inspirations that come, and see what shows up for us.

He has also learned to trust his inner guidance system. One summer day, a few Christian businesspeople met for lunch downtown. The lunch conversation turned to an absent fellow Christian who had left the church. One man began to cast judgment on him, and a few others joined in. My son began to feel heavy and very uncomfortable with the direction of the conversation, so he switched the discussion to a different topic, which brought back lightness and flow. The conversation had been flowing until judgment began. Judgment *always* stops flow. Trust your feelings of lightness or heaviness. That is God speaking to your soul through your conscience.

You may be wondering by now who I am. I have been informally studying the Bible for over forty years. Having said this, the Scriptures have truly only come alive for me these past few years *especially*. Verses that I read many times over the years now have a deeper and clearer meaning because I have experienced the power behind them. Having head knowledge of the Scriptures is no great feat; it is when we learn to *apply* this knowledge that true wisdom emerges.

I also perceive that I am a loving wife and a mom to four young adults, a people-development business co-owner, and someone whose faith was challenged as we went through this harrowing experience with our son that forced me to find answers. *I asked and it was given to me; I sought and found; I knocked and it was opened unto me.* Even though we sought answers from our external world at first, we were redirected back to the internal world, which we create through our thoughts and spoken words, and which is reinforced by belief or faith. The most incredible thing of all was that the answers were in front of me the whole time. I always knew faith was important, but I did not understand how powerful it was for everyday living. I believe faith is the answer to all of life's *real* questions.

Our souls came to this earth to fulfill a purpose. It is up to this human ego-based self to learn what that purpose is by tuning in to our inner energy and following its guidance through faith and inspiration. It is as we allow God to speak to us through our soul guidance that our conscience will lead us to our truth and purpose. God has made it easy for us to know what path to take, because He has put a hedge of thorns to mark our way. We know we are on the right path when we are in harmony and flow. If we hit thorns or roadblocks, perhaps we need to rethink our position and check in with our flowmeter. Where are we stuck? What do we need to relinquish and pass on in order to bring back flow? When we face tough experiences or illness, let us use these gifts as an opportunity for increased faith and abundance. It is when we learn not to attach negative ego emotion that we can truly soar through these experiences to higher faith and become completely enveloped in God's abundance of love and joy.

The *healing leaves* on the tree of life are truly a gift from God to all humankind for our living, health, and healing. However, let us not stop there. We all have the power, through faith, to raise our vibration level to even more elevated heights, from which we can partake of the *fruit* of the tree of life, where liberty, love, peace, and joy reign. Our divine team will lead us into all truth as we learn to recognize their guidance and follow our inspirations to greater abundance.

Bibliography

Foreword

1. Galatians 5:22–23
2. Revelation 2:7
3. This law originated in 1908. For more information, go to http://lawsoftheuniverse.weebly.com/law-of-corespondance.html.

Chapter 1

1. For more information, visit http://lawsoftheuniverse.weebly.com/law-of-vibration.html.
2. For more on this topic, go to http://www.abundance-and-happiness.com/quantum-physics.html.
3. For more about Bohr, visit http://www.livescience.com/32016-niels-bohr-atomic-theory.html.
4. To read more about the Copenhagen Interpretation, go to http://abyss.uoregon.edu/~js/21st_century_science/lectures/lec15.html.
5. Joe Dispenza, *You Are the Placebo: Making Your Mind Matter* (London: Hay House UK Limited, 2014).
6. Ibid.

7   Dr. Shad Helmstetter, What to Say When You Talk to Yourself, Pocket Books, Simon & Schuster, 1982
8   For more on this, see https://hiddenlighthouse.wordpress.com/category/law-of-vibration/.
9   For more about this, see http://www.drdomm.com/neurons-the-fire-together-wire-together/.

Chapter 2

1   Melody Beattie, *The Language of Letting Go* (Center City, MN: Hazelden,1990), 218.
2   See www.karmarescue.org/paws-for-life
3   See http://www.tainio.com/index.php?pageControl=about.
4   See http://www.zoominfo.com/p/Bruce-Tainio/6467701.
5   See http://www.tainio.com and http://justalist.blogspot.ca/2008/03/vibrational-frequency-list.html.
6   See http://web.archive.org/web/20100724091033/http://www.sangraal.com/rife.htm.
7   See http://greatist.com/health/ask-expert-will-eating-slowly-help-me-lose-weight.
8   For more information, go to http://theintentionexperiment.com/wp-content/uploads/2011/01/germination-experiment.pdf.

Chapter 3

1   *OxfordDictionaries.com*, s.v. "discernment," http://www.oxforddictionaries.com/definition/american_english/discernment.

Chapter 6

1. For more on this, watch the video here: https://www.youtube.com/watch?v=UkwU-A6aSSw.
2. Dr. Joe Dispenza, Neurosummit III, 2015.

Chapter 7

1. For more information on the law of cause and effect, visit http://lawsoftheuniverse.weebly.com/law-of-cause-and-effect.html.
2. See http://len.life/shows/the-aware-show/derek-rydall.

Chapter 8

1. For more information, see http://www.amberallen.com/personal-growth/law-detachment/.

Afterword

1. Dr. Joe Dispenza, *Breaking the Habit of Being Yourself* - Notes. Hay House Inc. 2012,315

About the Author

Lori Kostenuk is a new Canadian author with *The Laws of the Universe and the Bible: A Practical Guide to Abundant Living* being her first published book.

Lori currently resides in central Alberta, and is a paralegal by trade, an artist by talent, and an author by default. Lori is co-owner of an international people development company, specializing in workforce management, sales, productivity, and team behavioral science.

Lori and her husband raised their four children in a non-traditional Christian environment. Lori has been an informal student of the Bible for over forty years, and continues to be inspired by the wisdom it contains as life unfolds.

Made in United States
Orlando, FL
14 February 2024